BEADED
Adornment

BEADED
Adornment

JEANETTE SHANIGAN

krause publications

700 East State St., Iola, WI 54990-0001
Telephone 715-445-2214
www.krause.com

Photography by Ross Hubbard
Illustrations by Paison Productions
Book Design by Jan Wojtech

Acknowledgments

Many thanks to my beading students both past and present for being such willing "guinea pigs." Thank you to the Theiners for allowing me to teach at Frontier Imports. To Marcia for her extra help in chasing down just the right beads. Special thanks to my family -- Gordon, Donnavon and Shawn -- for their continued support and tolerance of my "bead habit"!

Like most beadwork artists, I have many books about beadwork. The books listed below, no doubt, influenced my techniques:

Blakelock, Virginia,
  Those Bad, Bad Beads
DeLong, Deon,
  Techniques of Beading Earrings
Schunzel, Veon,
  Creative Beaded Earrings
Starr, Sadie,
  Beading with Seed Beads, Gem Stones and Cabochons
Taylor, Carol,
  Creative Bead Jewelry
Wells, Carol Wilcox,
  Creative Bead Weaving
Williams, Gini,
  Beadz

I recommend these books for additional information and inspiration.

Library of Congress Cataloging-in-Publication Data

Shanigan, Jeanette L.
   Beaded Adornment/ Jeanette L. Shanigan
   p. 128 cm.
   ISBN 0-87341-585-X
      1. Beadwork.   2. Jewelry making.   I. Title.

CIP 97-80610

INTRODUCTION

I have intended for this book to be for the beginner *and* the experienced bead artist. Six of the most common beadwork techniques are clarified and illustrated. Each technique explanation precedes three to six projects. The projects vary in difficulty and complexity, the first project in each section being the easiest.

Like all beadwork artists, I have developed my own preferences, prejudices and idiosyncrasies. For example, I do not wax my thread; I am an ardent fan of Japanese beads, especially Delicas/antiques, I refuse to use plastic beads -- too tacky.

I firmly believe that if I intend to spend hours completing a piece, I ought to use materials that will enhance my labors. Who knows? Maybe I am creating a family heirloom or a great work of art! Although I have some personal opinions, I don't profess to have the definitive answers on the art of beadwork. Instead, I encourage you to find your own revelations through trial and error.

Beginners often seem disappointed with the caliber of their beadwork. This is always a surprise to me. Every other skill requires hours, even years of practice to achieve competency. Why shouldn't beadwork? It may be necessary to make several versions of the same project before the bead artist feels it is "perfect." Actually, Native Americans have the right idea with their spirit bead concept. The spirit bead is an *intentional* mistake in the beadwork to remind humankind that mere humans cannot expect to achieve perfection. So, don't focus on the mistakes; look at the skills attained and practice, practice, practice.

Finally, many of the illustrated examples appear very loose. Meaning, there is too much thread showing between the beads and stitches. This was necessary to show the movement of the needle and thread. Pull the beadwork tight while working, with little or no thread visible. Note: The abbreviation "N&T" means "needle and thread."

CONTENTS

PEYOTE STITCH TECHNIQUES -86

SPLIT-LOOM TECHNIQUES -104

GALLERY OF BEADWORK BY ALASKAN ARTISTS -118

ABOUT THE AUTHOR -128

PART ONE
MATERIALS

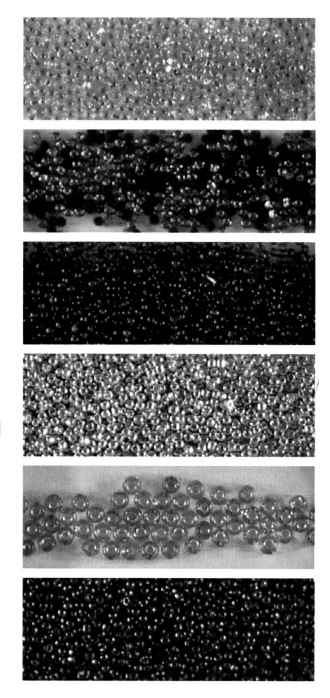

MATERIALS

Certain materials are essential to the beadworking process. This section describes materials necessary for general beadwork, as well as those required for the   projects in this book. Note that there is a list of specific, required materials at the beginning of each project.

BEADS

Beads come in a variety of shapes, sizes, colors and finishes. Beads may be made of glass, gemstones, metals, wood, shells, bone, clay or porcelain. The possibilities are endless. Regardless of the type of bead, a good rule of thumb is to purchase the best quality bead that you can afford. High quality beads will be more uniform in size, the holes will be larger and consistent in size and any surface finishes will be more durable. The classification of beads used in this book are: seed beads and accent beads.

SEED BEADS

I recommend Japanese or Czech seed beads for these projects. If given a choice between the two, choose the Japanese seed beads. The holes tend to be larger and sometimes that's a necessity, rather than a luxury. It is also important to consider surface finishes and glass types when selecting seed beads. Some beads tend to recede (transparent, matte), while others stand out (opaque, silver-lined, gilt-lined, iridescent, metallic) visually in the design. Achieve the best results by using bold and subtle beads. When selecting beads, consider both the accentuated design areas and colors. Color is another aspect to consider when selecting seed beads. Frankly, some people have a natural knack for selecting colors, while others could use a thorough course in color theory. Often the colors in the cabochon or accent beads can be an invaluable guide. Those selling their beadwork may want to consider Americans' favorite colors: blue, red, green, white, pink and purple. Sometimes, dare to be radical in your color selections; the results may be surprising!

ACCENT BEADS

A variety of beads, including Austrian Swarovski crystals, Czech glass, gemstone, Peruvian ceramic, wooden and mother-of-pearl, are to accent the beadwork. As with seed beads, consider quality, color and composition when selecting accent beads. Some patience and perseverance may also be necessary. Finding just the right accent bead is equivalent to finding just the right accessories for a new outfit. It takes time.

NEEDLES

I recommend English beading needles in sizes 10, 12 and 13. Provided that you use good quality beads, these needles should work for all projects. Use a larger size 10 needle when sewing through leather or UltraSuede. I suggest long 12's for loom beading.

THREAD

I recommend Nymo™ thread in sizes **B** and **D**. Some people advocate Kevlar™ thread, but watch out; it can cut itself. Buy the largest quantity of thread available. Thread wound on bobbins tends to knot, twist and tangle more than thread wound on cones. When threading the needle, begin threading with the first end off the cone, then cut to the appropriate length. A good length for beginners is 4-6 feet. To avoid adding thread and/or dealing with knots, experienced beadworkers may want to use more in some situations.

WAX

"Knot gremlins" are a reality in beadwork! People use a variety of techniques to avoid those undesired, dreaded knots that mysteriously appear. Some people use beeswax or candle wax to wax the thread. Others prefer to become adept at removing knots and use nothing, which eliminates wax residue. Still others take the middle road and use a thread conditioner, such as Thread Heaven™. Some people even press thread with an iron. Only trial and error will determine a personal knot solution.

FELT vs. INTERFACING

Felt is available in a wide range of colors and I suggest using it with the back stitch. Some people prefer interfacing (pellon), but it is only available in black and white. A good compromise is fusible interfacing ironed to felt.

SUEDE LEATHER vs. ULTRASUEDE™

I suggest a lightweight leather, but UltraSuede also works. Although leather is a bit more stiff, both seem equally difficult to sew, but using a size 10 needle helps.

CLEAR NAIL POLISH

Any inexpensive brand will do. I use nail polish to set knots, strengthen frayed thread and stiffen beadwork. Because it contains acetone, nail polish can affect surface finishes on beads. Always check for colorfastness before using polish!

GLUE

I recommend Bond 527™ for several reasons: it is clear, thus colors will not become distorted. Bond 527 is very effective on a wide variety of materials (i.e., glass, leather, stone, etc.). Finally, a stiff bond is formed (when a generous amount is used). This bond eliminates the necessity to use a piece of plastic between the beadwork and the leather backing (as some suggest). Always allow sufficient drying time.

HINTS FOR USING PORCUPINE QUILLS

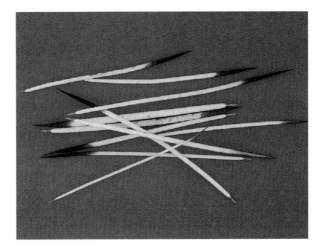

Porcupine quills add an interesting, natural touch to beadwork. However, quills do require special handling. My nieces and nephews, who live in Bush Alaska, often harvest quills from live animals for me. They use the towel trick, so as not to harm the animals. This trick is done by gently flicking a towel at a porcupine. A friend once harvested an entire road kill by stuffing it in a plastic bag, which in turn went in her freezer. Sometime later, she discovered that quills poke holes in plastic bags and the rather skunky smell had permeated her entire freezer. Dealing with frozen or fresh road kills is nasty! The moral -- don't be greedy; use the towel trick to harvest a few quills, and leave the rest for other scavengers!

ACQUISITION

Purchase porcupine quills at most bead/craft stores. "Harvest" quill from live animals or road kills. Painlessly accomplish this by gently flicking a bath towel at the animal. The quills will cling to the towel on contact. Discard any badly discolored or broken quills.

CLEANING

Natural quills are covered with animal dander and dirt and require washing before use. Soak the quills in a mixture of warm water and dishwashing detergent. Rinse well in warm water and dry on paper towels.

CUTTING

While the quills are still damp and flexible, cut off both sharp ends. Be careful! Trim ends away from your face and body. You might do the actual trimming inside a *clear* plastic bag or directly over the trash receptacle. Quills embedded in skin are painful and may cause infection.

STORAGE

Store quills in an airtight container. Keep container out of strong, direct light or sunlight.

USE

Cut the quills to the desired lengths. Use size 13 needles and **B** thread. Simply push the needle through the pithy center of the quill.

DYEING

Use a whole package, of commercial Rit-dye,™ to one or two quarts of water. Depending on desired color intensity, simmer quills for 15-30 minutes. Rinse quills in cold water.

FRAGILITY

Quills are extremely fragile and require TLC. To prevent splitting, coat the ends of the quills with clear nail polish. It helps to preserve the quills by applying a light coating of clear nail polish over their entire length. I do not recommend quills for an item that will endure a great amount of wear and tear, such as a belt buckle.

EQUIPMENT

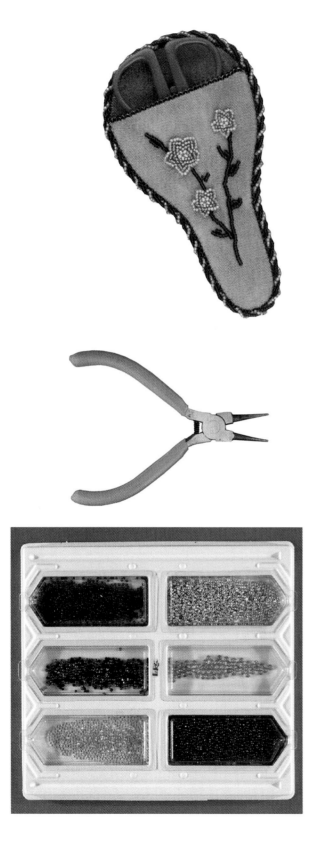

Possessing the right tools will contribute to the pleasure in beadworking. It's handy to store these items in a "toolbox" (cookie tin, plastic container, tackle box). When people ask me where I store my equipment and beads, I laugh and say "a bedroom." I do also have a large tackle box with three removable, compartmented utility boxes that I take on trips to shows, classes, etc. Since I store my beads in the same utility boxes, it's easy to interchange them. Actually, the storage system seems to be an indicator of the level of addiction! Beginners often use something handy, such as cookie tins. The moderately hooked will spend money on a storage system, i.e., a tackle box. The true addicts take over the spare bedroom and label it a studio and/or begin lobbying for an addition to the house.

SCISSORS

A good, sharp pair of scissors is essential. Almost any scissors will cut thread, but leather and felt require a sharp pair.

NAIL CLIPPERS

These are ideal for trimming thread or soft flex wire close to the beadwork.

PLIERS

A pair of needle-nose pliers is a necessity. If you live in an all-male household, purchase the daintiest, most delicate, pink-handled pliers available. Otherwise, pliers will "turn up" missing or greasy! As the budget allows, purchase round-nose pliers, crimping pliers and wire cutters, which are useful additions to a toolbox.

BEAD TRAYS

During the beadworking process, a "bead palette" will be essential. Some people make piles of beads on a piece of leather. Others use ceramic watercolor palettes. Still others recycle metal lids from jars, or plastic lids from potato chip, nut or yogurt containers. Another option is a plastic six-compartment tray, with lids and pouring spouts, designed especially for beads. Whatever your preference, check the depth of the container. If it is too deep, it will be difficult to pluck beads from the tray.

COLORED MARKERS

These are useful for coloring obvious threads, or designs and patterns.

RULER

Accurate measurements are a must. Usually a six-inch ruler is sufficient.

POST-IT-NOTES

These are superb for marking places on patterns. It is a good idea to note the individual bead colors on the post-it-note. For example, you will determine color **A** at a glance.

LOOM

Purchase or make a loom to create the loom beading. This loom can be easily constructed and will work nicely for the necklaces in this book.

One 25" x 7" x 3/4" board (base)
Two 4" x 7" x 3/4" boards (sides)
Eight wood screws (1 1/2-inch long)
Two medium nails (1 1/2-inch long)
Two 6-inch springs
Four wood screws (1/2-inch long)

Pound each nail into the exact center of the sides. The nail should protrude about 1 inch. Fasten the sides to the base with the longer wood screws. Attach the springs to the top of the sides with the shorter wood screws. If desired, sand the edges a bit.

WORK AREA

The location where a bead artist chooses to work is a matter of personal preference. Some artists prefer to work at the kitchen table. Others work in the living room and enjoy "quality time" with family members. Some artists enjoy a workroom or a studio. Some even bead in bed, and later tell hilarious stories of spouses waking up with stray beads embedded in cheeks, etc.! Regardless of the site, a few amenities will make the work area more productive.

LIGHTING

Adequate lighting is reasonably the most important consideration. Most desirable is a combination of natural and artificial light. Tired, strained eyes quickly turn beadwork into drudgery!

BEAD STORAGE

There are several possibilities for bead storage: fishing tackle boxes, embroidery floss organizers or cookie tins. Store beads in small, individual plastic bags within the larger containers. If purchasing beads on hanks, always remember to immediately retie the strings at the top. It's also nice to have a cabinet just for storing bead paraphernalia.

MAGNIFYING GLASS

Some people, especially beginners, discover that a magnifying glass is a necessity for threading beading needles or working with tiny, tiny beads. Others discover that the difficulty is not caused by the size of the beads and needles, but that a trip to the eye doctor has been too long procrastinated! Beadworking is definitely not an art in which there is room to be vain about wearing corrective lenses!

HAND VACUUM

Kids spill 'em, pets spill 'em, spouses spill 'em, even bead artists spill beads. A hand-held vacuum is a good way to retrieve the beads quickly and easily.

LAP TRAY

Look for the type with a pillow attached to the tray. These are remarkably stable and make beadworking possible during long vehicle trips or while commuting.

PART TWO
BACK STITCH
TECHNIQUES

BACK STITCH TECHNIQUES

Of all the beadworking stitches in this book, back stitch is most like hand-sewing or embroidery. It is often referred to as bead embroidery. The beads are initially sewn to some kind of fabric (felt, pellon or ultra-suede), then the beadwork is backed with leather or ultra-suede to hide the threads of the back stitching.

1. Thread the needle (size 12 or 13) with a single strand of **B** thread. Tie a knot in the end.

2. Bring the N&T from the back of the felt to the front, about half the width of the bead diameter from the cabochon or the last row of beads.

3. String four beads and push the beads down next to the point where the thread exits the felt.

4. Pass the N&T back through the felt. There should be NO thread showing between the beads.

5. Push the N&T back through the felt to the front between the second and third beads.

6. Pass the N&T through the third and fourth beads.

7. Repeat instruction numbers 3-6 until completing the entire row. Note that at the end it may be necessary to string fewer than four beads.

8. After completing a row, pass the N&T through all beads in the row. Give a slight tug to even or "round out" the row. I reference this step as "encircle" in the project directions.

9. Bring the N&T to the back of the felt. Repeat instruction numbers 2-8 to do another row.

10. After completing all the rows, bring the N&T to the back of the felt and tie a knot. Trim.

ADDING NEW THREAD

Simply bring the old thread to the back of the felt and knot. Tie a knot in the end of the new thread and push the N&T from the back to the front of the felt. If adding thread in the middle of a row, bring the N&T up through the last two beads in the row, then pass the N&T through the two beads. Continue with the back stitch.

TROUBLE-SHOOTING

1. Beadwork is bumpy -- Give beads plenty of room between the cabochons and the rows -- don't crowd them. Note step 2.

2. Thread shows between the beads -- The four beads need to be snug against each other before passing the N&T to the back of the felt. The needle also needs to be flush against the fourth bead. Note step 3.

3. Cabochon/concho falls off -- Use a generous amount of glue and dry on a flat surface 8-12 hours before handling.

1.

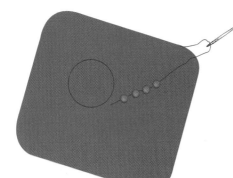

2.

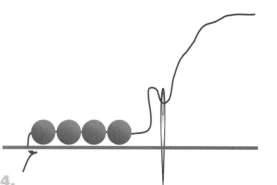

4.

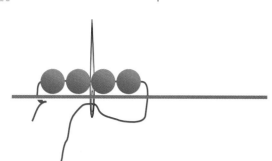

5.

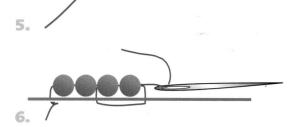

6.

TWISTED-EDGE CABOCHON SET

This is a striking, yet simple way to "frame" a particularly beautiful or interesting cabochon.

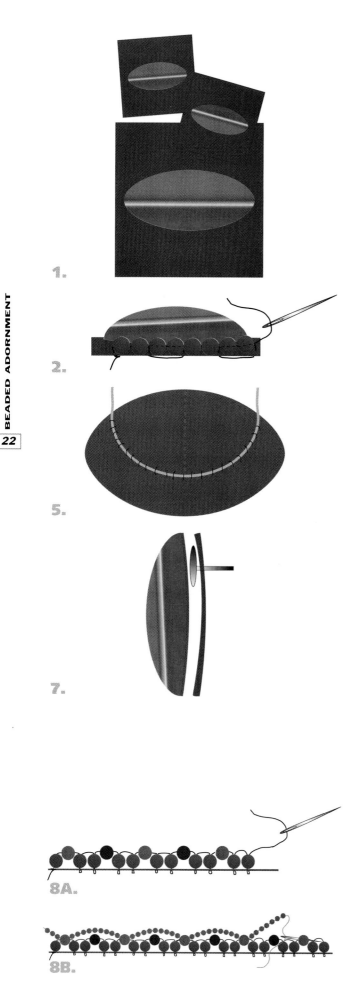

1.

2.

5.

7.

8A.

8B.

MATERIALS

ONE 25 x 30MM CABOCHON
TWO 10 x 15MM CABOCHONS
SEED BEADS, SIZE 11, 2 COLORS
40 6MM CZECH GLASS BEADS
EIGHT 4MM CZECH GLASS BEADS
ONE 6 x 6-INCH FELT SQUARE
NYMO THREAD: B & D
NEEDLES: 10 & 12
TIGER TAIL OR SOFT FLEX WIRE, .015
LEATHER SCRAP
BOND 527 GLUE
NECKLACE CLASP
TWO EAR POSTS

1. Cut three pieces of felt: one 4x4-inch piece and two 2x2-inch pieces.

Glue the cabochons onto the center of each piece of felt and allow to dry thoroughly.

2. Use a size 12 needle and a single, knotted strand of **B** thread.

Work four rows of back stitch around the large cabochon.

Do the first two rows in color A and the second two rows in color B. Be sure to "encircle" each row; that is, pass the N&T through the entire row again.

3. Leaving a 1/16-inch edge, carefully cut out each cabochon.

4. Cut ovals out of leather, the same size as each of the cabochons.

5. Cut a 24-inch piece of tiger tail. Place and position the tiger tail on the back of the large cabochon and baste it into place. Be sure that each end is the same length and that each side of the tiger tail is equal distance from the center point.

6. Use a generous amount of Bond 527 and glue the large leather oval to the back of the large cabochon.

Dry thoroughly.

7. Sandwiching an ear post in between, glue each small cabochon to a leather oval.

Allow to dry.

8. Do the edge beading around each cabochon. Note that the twisted edge is a 3-step process, as illustrated. Use a single, knotted strand of **D** thread and a size 10 needle.

a. (3-1-2-1-2--2)

b. Make loops (7-9 beads) between the color **B** extended (point) beads.

Make loops (7-9 beads) between the color A extended (point) beads.

c. Pass the N&T from the color A point bead THROUGH the color B loop into the next color A bead point.

Tie off, clip thread and hide knot.

9. String beads on each piece of tiger tail:

<blockquote>
one color **A**
three color **B**
one color **A**
three color **B**
one color **A**
one 4mm
one color **B**
one 6mm
one **B**
one 6mm
one **B**
one 6mm
one **B**
one 6mm
one **B**
one 6mm
one **B**
one 4mm.
</blockquote>

Repeat pattern again.

String:

<blockquote>
one **A**
three **B**
one **A**
three **B**
one **A.**
</blockquote>

Ten 6mm and alternate with one **B**.

String a crimp bead and pass the tiger tail through the necklace clasp. Pass back through the crimp bead and several beads. Be sure that wire is not showing between the beads. Close the crimp bead with crimping pliers and trim off the excess tiger tail. Repeat for the other side.

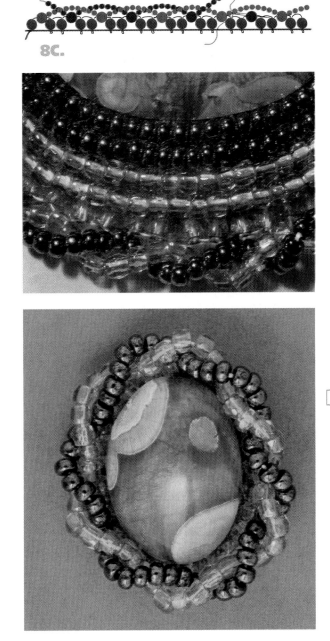

8C.

ANTIQUE-LOOK CAB-OCHON SET

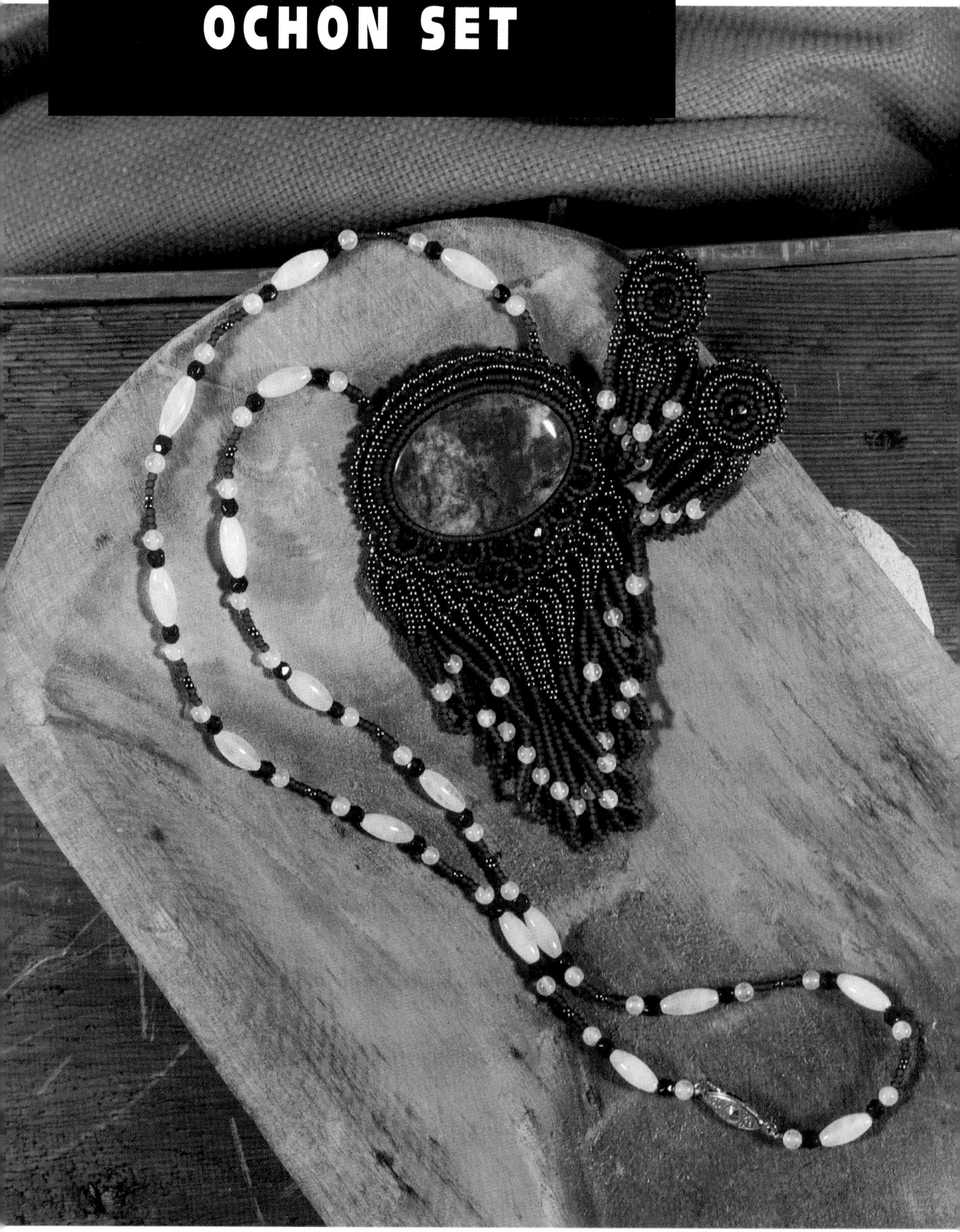

MATERIALS

BEADING NEEDLES: 10 & 12
NYMO THREAD: B & D
ONE 30 x 40MM OVAL CABOCHON
SEED BEADS, SIZE 11, TWO COLORS
44 4MM FACETED CZECH GLASS BEADS
61 4MM GEMSTONE BEADS
16 12MM OVAL GEMSTONE BEADS
ONE FELT SQUARE, 6 x 6-INCH
ONE YARD TIGER TAIL OR SOFT FLEX WIRE
TWO CRIMPING BEADS
ONE NECKLACE CLASP
TWO EAR POSTS
LEATHER SCRAP
BOND 527 GLUE

1. Cut three pieces of felt: one 4 x 4-inch piece and two 2 x 2-inch pieces.

2. Glue the cabochon in the center of the 4 x 4-inch felt square. Use a generous amount of glue and allow it to dry overnight on a flat surface.

3. Using a single, knotted strand of **B** thread and a size 12 needle, outline the cabochon with back stitch. Use seed beads, color **A**. When finishing this row and ALL subsequent rows, "encircle" the row. That is, pass the N&T once again through the entire row. This will even out the circle and reinforce the beadwork.

4. Measure the cabochon lengthwise and mark the center point on the felt. Sew a 4mm glass bead on this point next to the row of back stitching. Use back stitch to outline the glass bead on the three remaining sides with eight color **A** beads.

5. Continue adding and outlining beads in this manner on one side of the center 4mm bead. Complete four. Encircle all back stitching (as described in step 3). Add, outline and encircle three 4mm beads on the other side of the center bead.

6. Sew a 4mm glass bead below the center bead on the right. Outline it with six to seven color **A** seed beads. Repeat for the left side below the center 4mm bead. Encircle.

7. Sew a 4mm glass bead below the center bead between the two added in step 6. Outline the glass bead with five to six color **A** beads. Encircle.

8. Starting at one edge of the outlined 4mm glass beads, do back stitching to the other edge.

Pattern: three color **A**, two color **B**. Repeat.

9. Outline the entire edge with a row of color **B** back stitching.

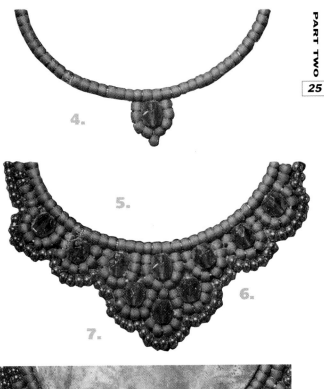

4.

5.

6.

7.

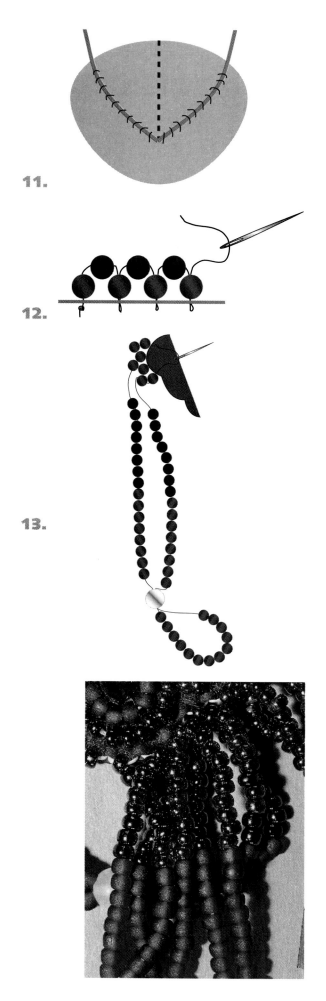

11.

12.

13.

10. Leaving a 1/16-inch edge, carefully cut out the beadwork.

11. Center the tiger tail (soft flex wire) on the back of the beadwork and baste it in place. Be sure the ends are equal distance from the center point. Glue a piece of leather to the back of the beadwork. Dry thoroughly on a flat surface. Trim away excess leather.

12. Using **D** thread and a size 10 needle, do edge beading around the beadwork. Start the edge beading approximately where the dangles will begin. If possible, use a LONG piece of thread. Complete the edge beading AND dangles without adding more thread. If desired, do the 4-3-2 edge around the top portion of the beadwork and the 3-2-1 edge around the bottom where the dangles will be located.

13. **Dangles** -- Bring the needle out through the desired point of the edge beading.

> String:
> > eight color **B**
> > eight color **A**
> > 4mm gemstone (or glass)
> > 13 color **A** beads.

Pass the N&T through the 4mm bead and string eight color **A** and eight color **B** beads.

Pass the N&T through the next point on the edge beading. Continue adding dangles until completing 19-20.

Note that each dangles increases (or decreases) by one color **B** and one color **A**. Tie off, trim thread and hide knot between felt/leather layers.

14. String each end of the tiger tail by repeating this pattern --

> three color **A**
> two color **B**
> three color **A**
> one 4mm gemstone
> one 4mm glass
> one 1" oval gemstone
> one 4mm glass
> one 4mm gemstone.

Each side should be 12-13 inches in length.

15. String a crimping bead. Thread the tiger tail through the necklace clasp, back through the crimping bead and through two-four beads. Pull the wire tight and close the crimping bead with crimping pliers. Trim off excess wire. Repeat for the other side.

EARRINGS

1. Sew a 4mm glass bead in the center of one 2 x 2-inch felt square.

2. Use the back stitch to outline the 4mm glass bead with three rows.

Row #1 = color **A**
Row #2 = two color **A** two color **B**
Row #3 = color **B**

3. Leaving a 1/16-inch edge, carefully cut out the beadwork. Cut a piece of leather the same size as the beadwork.

4. Placing an ear post in between, glue the beaded piece to the leather. Allow to dry.

5. Using **D** thread and a size 10 needle, do edge beading around the piece.

Start the edge beading where the dangles will begin.

6. Add dangles as in step13 above.

String:

five color **B**
five color **A**
4mm gemstone
seven color **A.**

Pass the N&T through the gemstone and string five color **A** and five color **B**.

Note that each dangle increases (or decreases) by one color B and one color A.

There should be five dangles.

7. Repeat for the other earring.

1.

4.

CONCHO
MEDALLION
SET

PART I: MEDALLIONS

LARGE MEDALLION

1. Using a glue gun, glue a large concho to a 4-inch felt square. Use Bond 527 glue to attach metal buttons to the felt.

2. Using **B** thread, do two rows of back stitch around the concho. Be careful to begin the second row with the placement of the single color **B** bead (centered above any two color **B** beads in row one). The intent of row 2 is to form color **B** points; if necessary, adjust the number of color **A** beads between the single color **B** beads.

First row: three color **A**, two color **B** (repeat)
Second row: one color **B**, five color **A** (repeat)

3. Sew a 6mm gemstone bead next to the second row of beads.

Outline it on the three exposed sides with ten to twelve color **A** beads.

Continue sewing gemstone beads and back stitch with seed beads until completing 12 sets.

4. Sew a color **B** crystal between each gemstone bead set.

5. Cut out the medallion. Cut close to the edge, but be careful not to cut the threads.

2A.

2B.

3B.

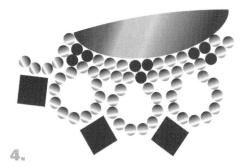

4.

6. Use a glue gun (or Bond 527) to glue each concho to a 3-inch felt square.

7. Back stitch a row around the concho: three color **A**, two color **B** (repeat).

8. Sew a 4mm gemstone bead next to the row of beads. Outline the three exposed sides with eight to nine color **A** beads. Continue and complete 12 sets.

9. Sew a color **B** bead between each gemstone bead set.

10. Carefully cut out the medallions.

PART II:
DANGLES AND STRINGING

11. Cut two 30-inch pieces of tiger tail (soft flex).

12. Position the tiger tail on the back of the large medallion and attach it by basting through the felt across the tiger tail. Be sure that each side of the tiger tail is equal distance from the center point. Use Bond 527 to glue a piece of leather to the back of the medallion. Dry thoroughly on a flat surface. Trim the leather.

13. Using **D** thread and a size 10 needle, do edge beading with color **A** beads around the medallion. Start the edge beading approximately where the dangles will begin.

(3-2-2-1)

14. Bring the needle out through a point of the edge beading, string:

> three color **A**
> one color **C**
> three color **B**
> one color **C**
> one crystal
> one cylinder (bugle)
> one crystal
> one color **C**
> five color **A**
> one 6mm
> five color **A**.

Pass the needle through the:

> color **C**
> crystal
> cylinder
> crystal.

Then string:

> one color **C**
> three color **B**
> one color **C**
> three color **A**.

Pull the dangle tight and pass the needle through the next edge beading point. Continue adding until completing 13-14 dangles.

Increase (or decrease) each dangle by one color **A** and one color **B** bead.

15. String about 1 1/2 inches of beads on each piece of tiger tail. Duplicate the dangle pattern or create a new one.

16. Position the small medallions across the tiger tail and baste through the felt across the tiger tail.

17. Glue leather to the back of the small medallions. Dry thoroughly on a flat surface. Trim the leather.

18. Do edge beading around the small medallions.

19. String beads (to the desired length) on each piece of tiger tail. String a crimping bead. Thread the tiger tail through the necklace clasp, back through the crimping bead and through several beads. Pull the tiger tail tight, so there's no space between the beads. Close the crimping bead with crimping pliers and trim off the excess tiger tail. Continue until completing all four pieces.

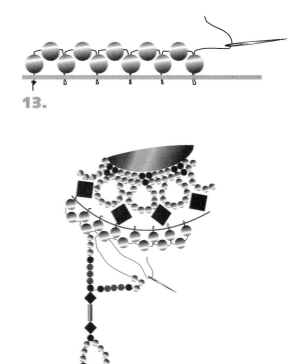

13.

14.

PART III: MATCHING EARRINGS

Use the 5/8-inch conchos and the 3mm beads to make matching earrings. Use the small medallion pattern. Sandwich earring posts between the leather backing and the felt and glue with Bond 527 glue. Do edge beading around each medallion and add dangles, if desired.

"WOVEN"
QUILL SET

MATERIALS

THREAD: NYMO B AND D
NEEDLES: 13 AND 10
80 8MM RICE BEADS
SEED BEADS, 2-CUTS, SIZE 11, ONE COLOR
EIGHT PORCUPINE QUILLS, 1 1/2-INCH LONG
6 x 6-INCH FELT SQUARE
LEATHER SCRAP
NECKLACE CLASP
TIGER TAIL OR SOFT FLEX WIRE, 1 YARD
TWO CRIMPING BEADS
TWO EAR POSTS
BOND 527 GLUE

PART I: NECKLACE

1. Clean and cut the quills. Cut the dark tips into 1/2-inch pieces. Use the remainder to cut 16 pieces that are each 5/8-inch in length. Note the hints for using quills in chapter one.

2. Cut the felt into a 4 x 4-inch piece and two 2 x 2-inch pieces.

3. Using a single, knotted strand of **B** thread and a 13 needle, sew a rice bead to the center of the large piece of felt.

4. Do three rows of back stitch around the rice bead. Be sure to "encircle" each row when finishing.

5. Sew eight pieces of the plain quill around the beadwork as indicated.

6. Sew down the remaining eight plain pieces of quill.

7. Sew on the dark-tipped quills.

8. Work three rows of back stitch around the quills.

9. If desired, sew a single bead to the felt between each set of quills.

10. Leaving a 1/16-inch edge, carefully cut out the beadwork.

11. Use the beadwork as a pattern to cut a piece of leather.

12. Fold the tiger tail in half. Smear the back of the leather with a generous amount of glue. Position the tiger tail in the center of the back. Top with the beadwork. Allow to dry on a flat surface.

13. Using **D** thread and a 10 needle, do 3-2-2-1 edge beading around the entire necklace pendant. Remember to start the edge beading about where the dangles will begin.

3.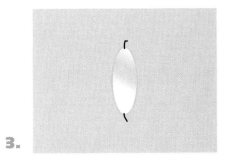

4.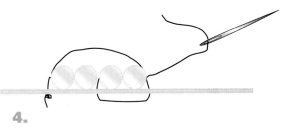

14.

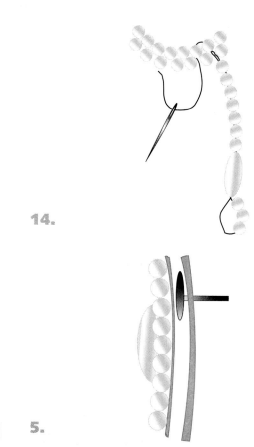

5.

14. String the dangles, noting that these do NOT hang from the point beads of the edging.

String:

> seven beads
> one rice
> three beads.

Pass the N&T through the rice bead, the seven beads, as well as through the back side of the edge bead.

Pass the N&T down through the next edge bead and string another dangle. Note that each dangle increases (or decreases) by three beads and a rice bead. There should be nine dangles.

15. Tie off, trim the thread, and hide the knot.

16. String each side of the tiger tail with 22 sets of three beads and one rice bead. String a crimping bead and the necklace clasp. Pass the tiger tail back through the crimping bead and several other beads. Pull it tight and close the crimping bead. Trim the excess wire. Repeat for the other side.

PART II: EARRINGS

1. Sew a rice bead to the center of each of the 2 x 2-inch pieces of felt.

2. Do three rows of back stitch around the rice bead.

3. Leaving a 1/16-inch edge, carefully cut out the beadwork.

4. Cut a leather backing the same size as the beadwork.

5. Sandwich earring posts between the leather backing and the beadwork and glue with a generous amount of Bond 527. Dry.

6. Do edge beading around the earrings and add dangles as in instruction numbers 13-15 above. Do three OR five dangles, as desired.

BUTTERFLY CABOCHON SET

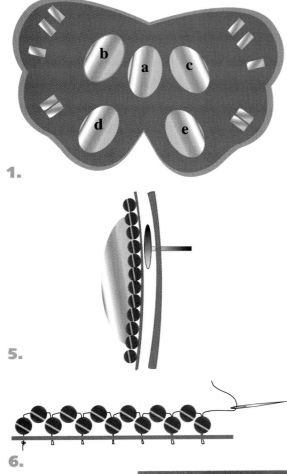

1.

5.

6.

MATERIALS

THREAD: NYMO B & D
NEEDLES: 10 & 12
SEVEN 15 X 20MM CABOCHONS
35 2 X 4MM GEMSTONE CYLINDERS
54 6MM GEMSTONE BEADS
SEED BEADS, 2-CUTS, SIZE 11, ONE COLOR
FELT
LEATHER SCRAP
TWO EAR POSTS
NECKLACE CLASP
TWO CRIMPING BEADS
ONE YARD TIGER TAIL OR SOFT FLEX WIRE
BOND 527 GLUE

1. Cut three pieces of felt: one 4x4-inch piece and two 2x2-inch pieces.

Trace the butterfly template on the larger piece of felt.*

Glue the middle cabochon (a) onto the felt as indicated.

Glue a cabochon onto each of the smaller pieces of felt. Allow to dry.

2. Use the back stitch to outline each of the cabochons. As you finish each cabochon, be sure to "encircle" the row; that is, pass the N&T through the entire row again.

3. Glue cabochons **b** & **c** onto the larger felt piece. Allow to dry.

4. Meanwhile, leaving a 1/16-inch edge, carefully cut out around each earring cabochon.

Cut two more ovals out of leather the same size as the beaded piece.

5. Sandwiching an ear post in between, glue each beaded piece to a leather oval. Dry.

6. Do 3-2-2-1 edge beading around each earring.

7. Continue with the butterfly and outline cabochons b & c with two rows of back stitching. "Encircle."

8. Glue on cabochons **d** & **e**. Allow to dry.

9. Outline cabs **d** & **e** with two rows of back stitch.

10. Use the back stitch to outline the entire butterfly shape.

11. Attach the cylinders and outline with back stitching.

12. Fill in the remaining exposed felt with back stitch. DON'T CROWD IT! Good back stitch should be flat, not bumpy.

13. Leaving a 1/16-inch edge, carefully cut out the butterfly.

14. Fold the tiger tail (soft flex) in half. Center the wire on the back of the butterfly and baste into place.

15. Glue the butterfly to a piece of leather. Dry thoroughly on a flat surface.

16. Cut out the butterfly. Starting at the lower center, use **D** thread and a size 10 needle and do 3-2-2-1 edge beading around the entire butterfly.

17. Work the dangle off two center beads of the edge beading.

String:
> 12 2-cuts
> one cylinder
> one 2-cut
> 6mm
> one 2-cut
> 6mm
> three 2-cuts.

Pass the N&T through the 6mm and the cylinder.

String 12 2-cuts and pass the N&T through the edge beading.

Take a stitch in the leather to secure, then knot and trim thread.

18. String each side of the tiger tail with 6mm, cylinders, and 2-cuts (pattern = 2-cut, 6mm, 2-cut, 6mm, 2-cut, cylinder, 2-cut) until you reach the desired length.

19. String a crimping bead. Pass the tiger tail through the hole on one end of the clasp and back through the crimping bead and at least one 6mm bead. Pull tightly, then use crimping pliers to close the crimp bead. Trim any excess wire.

*Enlarge the butterfly template, page 36, #1, by 50%, or decrease the photo, page 35, by 50%.

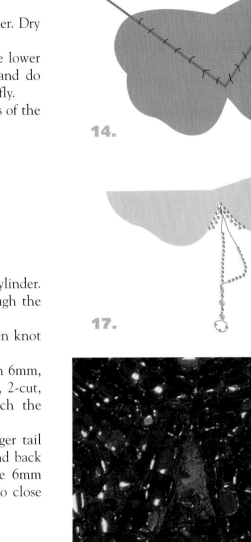

14.

17.

PART THREE
NETTING
TECHNIQUES

NETTING TECHNIQUES

Netting is a technique that results in a lacy, open weave. Netting can be done from top-to-bottom or from side-to-side and/or vertically or horizontally. The shape of the mesh and consequently, the beadwork can be changed by varying the number, size and type of beads used.

1. Begin by stringing the indicated number of beads or making a bead chain. This functions as the base row and part or all of the netting will be anchored off of this row.

2. Next, string the indicated number of beads and pass the N&T through the designated anchor bead in the base row.

3. Continue HORIZONTAL netting in this manner row-by-row until reaching the desired length. At the beginning of each new row, it will be necessary to pass the N&T through a certain number of beads to get to the first designated anchor bead.

4. Begin VERTICAL netting by stringing the entire bead length of the piece. A designated set of beads function as turn-beads. String more beads to these and anchor at various points on this row of turn beads. Finally, anchor the string to the base row.

ADDING NEW THREAD

Use the end of the old thread and the end of the new thread and tie a square knot as close as possible to the last bead on the old thread. Put a very small dab of clear nail polish on the knot. Put a needle on each end and work the tails into the beadwork for a half-inch or so. NEVER cut the threads at the knot! Clip off loose ends.

TROUBLE-SHOOTING

1. **Thread shows in the netting** -- Not enough beads were strung OR the work was not pulled tight after each bead addition.

2. **Bigger holes in the mesh** -- Too many beads were added or anchor beads were skipped. OR, the N&T was NOT passed through the designated number of beads to get into position to start a new row.

3. **The pattern is off** -- Use a post-it-note or ruler to mark each row in the pattern AND/OR remember the beginning of each new row shifts by one mesh.

1 & 2.

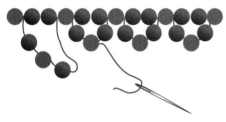

3.

4.

NETTED CHOKER SET

2.

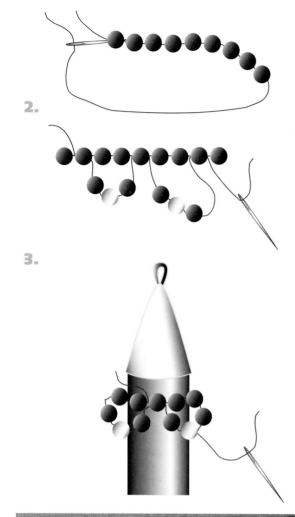

3.

THREAD: NYMO D
NEEDLES: 12
CORD, 5/32 IN DIAMETER, 17 INCHES LONG
SEED BEADS, SIZE 11, TWO COLORS
FOUR ROUND, FLAT SILVER BEADS, 3/4-INCH
    DIAMETER
ONE ROUND, FLAT SILVER BEAD, 1-INCH
    DIAMETER
EIGHT 4MM CZECH GLASS BEADS
TWO 6MM CZECH GLASS BEADS
FOUR HEAD PINS
TWO BELL CAPS
ONE BARREL CLASP
TWO EAR WIRES

A   *E*

PART I: CHOKER

1. Put a piece of cellophane tape on each end of the cord to prevent fraying. Cut the head off a head pin, push the pin halfway through the cord (1/4-inch from end) and twist one end of the pin around the cord several times. Push a bell cap over the other end of the head pin. Use round-nose pliers to form a loop in the head pin. Repeat for the other end of the cord.

2. Using a single, unknotted strand of thread, string nine color **A** beads.

Leaving a 6-inch tail, pass the N&T through the nine beads to form a circle.

Place the circle of beads around the cord next to a bell cap.

Tie a square knot and pass the N&T through the nearest bead.

3. String one **A**, one **B**, and one **A** bead, skip two beads and pass the N&T through the third bead.

Continue stringing one **A**-one **B**-one **A**.

Pass the N&T through every third bead until completing three loops.

Pass the N&T through the first TWO beads of the first loop.

4. Cover the entire cord with netting using this pattern:

       nine rows of **A-B-A**
       four rows of **A-A-A**

Repeat 14 times and end with nine rows of **A-B-A.**

5. Do one row of **A-A-A** netting.

Place two **A** between each center bead.

Stitch through the cord and back into the beads a couple of times to secure the beadwork.

Tie off in the beadwork and trim the thread.

6. Put a needle on the loose tail at the other end, stitch through the cord and back into the beads. Tie off.

7. Determine the location for the large-bead dangles.

Using a knotted strand of thread, sew through the cord to the location for the first dangle.

Pass the N&T through a bead, then string:

> three **A**
> one **B**
> three **A**
> Czech
> silver
> Czech
> three **A**.

Pass the N&T through the Czech, silver, and Czech.

String 3A, 1B, and 3A and pass the N&T through another bead on the choker.

Repeat for the other two dangles.

8. Tie off the thread in the beadwork and trim.

9. Attach a barrel clasp to the head pin loops.

PART II: EARRINGS

1. String a 4mm Czech, Flat silver, and a 4mm Czech bead on a head pin.

Trim the length, if necessary, then use round-nose pliers to make a loop in the head pin.

2. Attach ear wires.

NETTED BEZEL
CABOCHON SET

MATERIALS

THREAD: NYMO B
NEEDLES: 13
ONE 20 X 30MM CABOCHON
TWO 15 X 20MM CABOCHONS
56 6MM GEMSTONE BEADS
SEED BEADS, JAPANESE: SIZE 14, ONE COLOR
SMALL SCRAP OF LEATHER
TIGER TAIL OR SOFT FLEX WIRE, 24 INCHES
TWO CRIMPING BEADS
NECKLACE CLASP
TWO EARRING WIRES
BOND 527 GLUE

PART I: NECKLACE

1. Use a single, unknotted strand of thread to string 64 seed beads.

Leaving a 4-inch tail, pass the N&T through the 64 beads to form a circle.

Tie a square knot and bring the N&T out the nearest bead.

2. String seven beads, skip three beads, and pass the N&T through the 4th bead of the bead circle.

Continue stringing seven beads and passing the N&T through every fourth bead until 16 points have been formed.

3. Bring the N&T out the CENTER (fourth) bead of the nearest point.

String five beads.

Pass the N&T through the CENTER (fourth) bead of the NEXT point.

Repeat 15 more times.

4. Bring the N&T out the center (third) bead of the nearest five-bead point.

Strings three beads and pass the N&T through the center bead of the next point.

Repeat 15 more times. Work this row loosely; there will be thread showing.

5. Center the cabochon on the beadwork and pull the thread to gather the beads around the cabochon. Reinforce the last netted row by passing the N&T through all the beads again. At this stage little or no thread should be showing in the last row.

6. Weave the thread to the knot, tie another square knot, dab with polish and trim.

7. Firmly press the back side of the cabochon into a leather scrap. Use the indentation marks as a pattern to cut an oval the size of the UNBEADED part of the back of the cabochon.

8. Push the tiger tail through the netting across the back of the cabochon. Position in center.

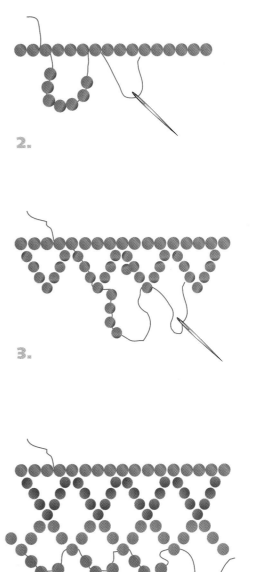

2.

3.

4.

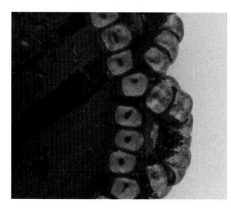

9. On one side of the tiger tail string one seed bead and one 6mm bead. Repeat this step 27 more times.

String a crimping bead and the necklace clasp.

Pass the tiger tail back through the crimping bead and a 6mm bead. Pull it tightly and close the crimping bead with crimping pliers.

Trim the excess tiger tail.

10. Repeat step 9 for the other side.

11. To hide the exposed tiger tail, glue the leather oval on the back of the cabochon.

PART II: EARRINGS

1. Make a circle of 36 beads as described in step 1.

2. Do three netted rows as described in steps 2, 3 and 4, except there will be nine points.

3. Center the cabochon in the beadwork. Be sure to center one of the points with the top of the cabochon. Continue as in step 5.

4. Weave the N&T to the single bead that connects the seven-bead and the five-bead points at the top of the cabochon.

String five beads and pass the N&T through the opposite side of the bead to form an ear wire loop.

Reinforce.

5. Weave the N&T to the knot and tie another knob. Dab with polish and trim.

6. Attach an ear wire.

7. Repeat for the other earring.

NETTED BEZEL "Y" NECKLACE AND EARRINGS

MATERIALS

Nymo™ thread, D
Needles: size 12 or 10
Three cabochons, 15 x 20mm and/or
    20 x 25mm
Delica™ beads: one color (metallics
    create a nice chain)
21 accent beads: metallic, stone,
    crystal, etc.
Two bead tips
One barrel clasp
Two ear wires
Note that the numbers in parentheses
    refer to the larger cabochons.

Part I: Necklace

1. Use a single, unknotted strand of thread.
String 32 (40) Delica beads.
Leave a six-inch tail, pass the N&T through the 32 (40) beads to form a circle.
Tie a square knot and pull the N&T out the nearest bead.

2. String five (seven) beads, skip three beads and pass the N & T through the fourth bead of the circle.
Continue to string five (seven) beads.
Pass the N & T through every fourth bead until eight (ten) points have been formed.

3. Bring the N & T out the **center** bead of the nearest point.
String five beads.
Pass the N & T through the **center** bead of the **next** point.
Repeat seven (nine) more times.

4. Bring the N & T out the center bead of the nearest five-bead point.
String three beads and pass the N & T through the center bead of the next point.
Repeat seven (nine) more times.
Note: Work this row loosely, thread will show.

5. Center the cabochon on the beadwork.
Pull the thread to gather the beads around the cabochon.
Reinforce the last netted row by passing the N&T through all the beads again.
Note: At this point, there should be no thread showing in the last row.

6. Weave the N&T to the centered hanger bead.
    String:
        ten Delicas
        three accent beads

2.

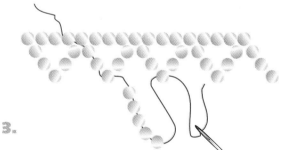

3.

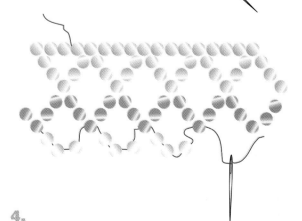

4.

ten Delicas
three accent beads
30 Delicas
three accent beads
150 Delicas
bead tip and one Delica.

7. Pass the N&T back through the bead tip and pull the strung beads taut.

Pass the N&T back through **all** the strung beads **and** through the centered bead on the cabochon.

8. String ten Delica beads and pass the N&T through the three accent beads.

9. String:
ten Delicas
three accent beads
30 Delicas
three accent beads
150 Delicas
bead tip and one Delica.

10. Pass the N&T back through the bead tip, through all the strung beads **and** the centered bead on the cabochon.

11. Weave the N&T to the loose tail and tie a square knot. Dab the knot with nail polish. Allow polish to dry and trim.

12. Attach the barrel clasp.

PART II: EARRINGS

1. Make a circle of 32 (40) beads as described in step 1 above.

2. Do three netted rows as described in steps 2, 3 and 4 above.

3. Center the cabochon in the beadwork.

Center one of the points with the top of the cabochon.

Continue as in step 5 above.

4. Weave the N&T to the single bead that connects the seven-bead and the five-bead points at the top of the cabochon.

String:
ten Delicas
three accent beads
six Delicas.

5. Reinforce the six Delicas by passing the N&T back through the six Delicas.

Note: Make sure this top loop is taut.

6. Pass the N&T through the three accent beads and string ten Delicas.

7. Pass the N&T through the center bead.

Weave to the loose tail and tie off.

Dab with nail polish, allow polish to dry and trim.

8. Repeat for a second earring.

9. Attach ear wires.

LEATHER AMULET BAG WITH NETTED BEZEL AND EARRINGS

MATERIALS

Nymo thread, B & D
Needles, size 10 or 12
Lightweight leather scrap
One 30 x 40mm cabochon
Seed beads, size 11, one or two colors
Four or five different accent beads
        (Czech glass, stone ovals & 4mm round,
        mini-donuts)
Soft flex wire, one yard
Bond 527™ glue
One necklace clasp
Two crimp beads

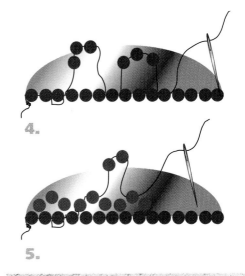

4.

5.

PART I: AMULET BAG

1. Trace the pattern on the leather scrap. Cut out the pattern pieces. See page 61 for pattern template.

2. Position the cabochon on the amulet bag flap. Lightly glue the cabochon in place.

3. Use a single strand of knotted **B** thread.

4. Work one row of back stitch around the cabochon. There should be 84 beads in this row (or another multiple of three).

"Encircle" the row.

5. Bring the N&T through any bead in the back stitch row.

String three beads and pass the N&T through the third bead.

Continue stringing three beads and passing through every third bead until there are 28 points (or the multiple divided by three).

6. Bring the N&T through the nearest center bead of a point.

String two beads and pass the N&T through the next point.

Continue placing beads between all points. It may be necessary to place only one bead between the points of the four corners. This will depend on the height of the cabochon.

7. Reinforce the two-bead row. Weave the N&T to the back-stitch row, go through the leather and tie off.

8. Form the bag by positioning the small piece of leather over the larger. Begin edge beading at the **X** and use the 3-2-1 edge to stitch the two pieces together. This also creates the decorative edge.

9. Count the number of spaces between beads, on the edge from the **X**, to the same point on the other side. This will determine the number of dangles.

10. String the dangles between the points on the edge.

String:

24 beads

one 4mm

11 beads.

Pass the N&T through the 4mm and string 24 beads.

Pass the N&T through the next edge point.

Note: Each dangle will increase (or decrease) by two beads. Options: String mini-donut on with the 11 beads. If desired, string the three accent dangles after all the others have been strung.

Space evenly from the center and tie off.

11. Punch four holes in the leather for the necklace chain: two marks are on the pattern and two will be located next to the edge beading.

Thread one end of the soft flex wire down through the hole near the edge, then up through the next hole.

String beads (length to the next hole).

Pass the wire down through the third hole and up through the last hole near the edge.

12. String beads on the soft flex wire (pattern = your choice).

String a crimping bead and the necklace clasp.

Pass the wire back through the crimping bead and, if possible, a couple of other beads. Close the crimping bead with crimping pliers.

Repeat for the other side.

13. *Optional: Glue an oval and small pieces of leather over the back stitching and the wire on the back side of the flap. Note: This is for reinforcement and aesthetic purposes.*

PART II: EARRINGS

1. Use a single, unknotted strand of **D** thread, string six seed beads. Leave a 4-inch tail.

To form a loop, pass the N&T through all six beads.

2. String:

4mm glass

4mm stone

oval stone

4mm stone

6mm glass

4mm stone

11 seed and one mini-donut.

3. Pass the N & T through the large beads and the six-bead loop.

4. Use the loose tail and the N & T to tie off.

Dab knot with nail polish, allow to dry and trim.

5. Repeat for the other earring.

6. Attach ear wires.

FEATHERS GALORE
STRIPED AMULET BAG
AND EARRINGS

MATERIALS

Nymo™ thread, D
Needle: size 12
Seed beads, size 11: two colors
Accent beads: 4mm Czech glass
      (fifty color A, 125 color B); seven large
      porcelain, glass or stone;
      twenty-one 6mm metal
20 metal feathers
Two head pins
Two ear wires

Part I: Amulet Bag

1. Use a single, unknotted strand of thread.
String 60 color **A** beads.
Use a square knot and tie the beads in a circle.
Pass the N&T through the first two beads.
Put the circle of beads around a paper roll.

2. Pick up three **A** beads, skip two beads and pass the N&T through the fifth bead (from the knot) in the circle.

3. Pick up three more **A** beads and pass the N&T through the eighth bead. Continue adding three beads in this manner until finishing the entire row.

At the end of the row pass the N&T through the **second bead** again, **and** through the **first two beads** of the first loop.

4. Pick up three **A** bead and pass the N&T through the center bead of the next loop. Continue adding sets of three beads until finishing the entire row.

At the end of the row, remember to pass the N&T through the first two beads of the first loop.

5. Follow the above row pattern.
Continue adding rows to complete the bag:
      one more row color **A**
      one row **A-B-A**
      two rows **B**
      five rows **A**
      one row **A-B-A**
      two rows **B**
      five rows **A.**

6. To close the bottom of the bag, align the center beads of each loop and stitch together.

7. Create 19 dangles: The N&T should come out the last center bead.
String:
      eight **A**
      two **B**
      one **A**
      two **B**

A Czech glass
B Czech glass
A Czech glass
five **B**
feather
five **B.**

Pass the N&T back through the three Czech glass. String:

two **B**
one **A**
two **B**
eight **A.**

Pass the N&T through the next center bead on the bottom of the bag. Continue adding each dangle in this manner. *Note: Each dangle increases (or decreases) by two* **A** *beads.*

8. **Create the closure flap:** Weave the N&T to the top row of the bag.

Pass the N&T through beads in the top row until the N&T is exiting the eleventh bead from the side. String:

eight **A**
B Czech glass
metal
B Czech glass
large accent (*continued on next page*)

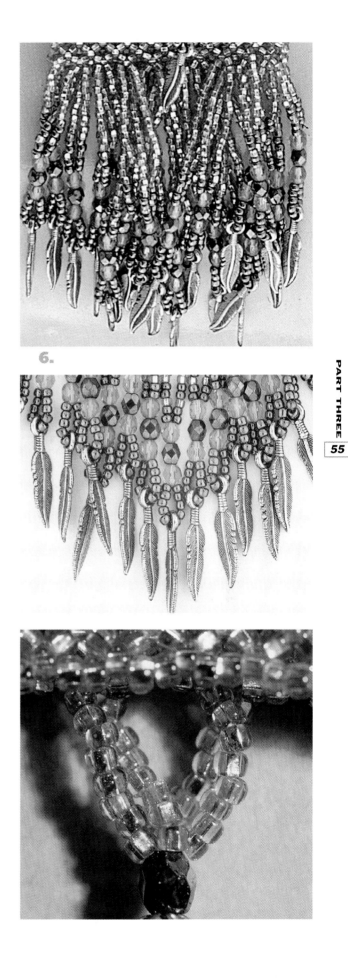

6.

B Czech glass
five **B**
feather
five **B**.

Pass the N&T back through all the large beads, then string eight **A** beads.

Pass the N&T through beads #15 and 14 on the top row.

String eight **A** and again pass the N&T through all the large beads, through the feather loop and back through the large beads.

String eight **A** and pass the N&T through bead #12 on the top row.

9. **String the neck chain**: Weave the N&T to the top side of the bag.

String this sequence of large beads:
> Czech glass
> large accent
> Czech glass
> metal
> Czech glass
> metal
> Czech glass
> metal
> Czech glass
> metal
> Czech glass
> metal
> Czech glass,
> metal
> Czech glass
> large accent
> Czech glass.

Czech glass = four **B**-**A**-**B**-**A**-four **B**
large accent = accent-**B**-metal-**B**-accent
metal = metal-**B**-metal-**B**-metal

10. Pass the N&T through the **A** bead at the other side of the bag.

To reinforce, pass the N&T through all beads in the neck chain.

11. Weave the thread into the bag and tie off.

Part II: Earrings

1. String:
> B Czech glass
> large accent
> B Czech glass
> metal.

B Czech glass on a head pin.

Use round-nose pliers to make a loop in the head pin.

2. Repeat for the other earring.

3. Attach ear wires.

BUGLE
COLLAR SET

MATERIALS

THREAD: NYMO D
NEEDLES: 12
SEED BEADS, ONE COLOR, SIZE 11
140 12MM BUGLE BEADS
200 4MM FACETED CZECH GLASS BEADS
ONE BARREL CLASP
TWO EAR WIRES

PART I: CHAIN

1. String:
> six beads
> half of the barrel clasp
> six beads
> one 4mm bead.

Leaving a 4-inch tail of thread, pass the N&T through all the beads to form a circle.

Use the loose tail and the N&T to tie a square knot.

2. Pass the N&T through the 4mm bead.

3. String:
> four beads
> one 4mm bead
> four beads.

4. Pass the N&T through the 4mm bead in the first circle, then through four beads and the 4mm bead in the second circle.

5. Repeat steps 3 and 4 until 61 circles have been done.

6. String six beads, half of the barrel clasp, and six beads.

Pass the N&T through the 4mm bead of the 61st circle. Then pass the N&T through the next ten beads on the 62nd circle.

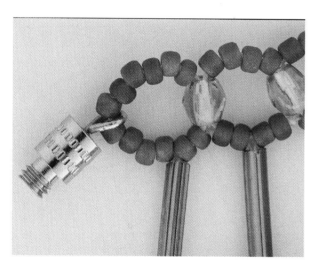

PART II: BUGLE NETTING

7. String:
> one bugle
> four beads
> one 4mm
> eight beads
> one bugle
> one 4mm
> three beads.

Pass the N&T through the 4mm and the bugle. String eight beads, one 4mm, and four beads and pass the N&T through the bugle bead.

8. Pass the N&T through the next four seed beads on the chain.

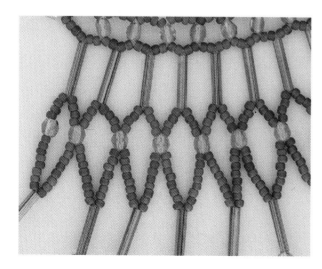

9. String one bugle and four beads.

Pass the N&T through the 4mm bead.

String eight beads, one bugle, one 4mm, and three beads.

Pass the N&T through the 4mm and the bugle.

String eight beads, one 4mm, and four beads.

Pass the N&T through the bugle bead.

10. Repeat steps 8 and 9 until netting is complete on the entire chain. Pull the beadwork tight after each addition of beads.

11. Tie off, dab clear nail polish on knots, and weave the loose ends into the beadwork.

PART III: EARRINGS
(USE THE NETTING AND THE BRICK STITCH)

1. Leaving a 4-inch tail and using an unknotted, single strand of thread, do a row of Commanche ladder with bugle beads, five bugles wide. Reinforce the row by passing the N&T back through the bugles to the first bugle.

2. String:

>   four beads
>   one 4mm
>   eight beads
>   one bugle
>   one 4mm
>   three beads.

Pass the N&T through the 4mm and the bugle.

String:

>   eight beads
>   one 4mm
>   four beads.

Pass the N&T through the second bugle of the bugle row.

3. Weave the N&T so it's coming out the bottom of the fourth bugle of the bugle row.

(This is easiest by simply looping through the threads at the top of the bugle row.)

String four beads and pass the N&T through the 4mm bead.

String:

>   eight beads
>   one bugle
>   one 4mm
>   three beads.

Pass the N&T through the 4mm and the bugle. String eight beads, one 4mm, and four beads.

Pass the N&T through the fifth bugle of the bugle row.

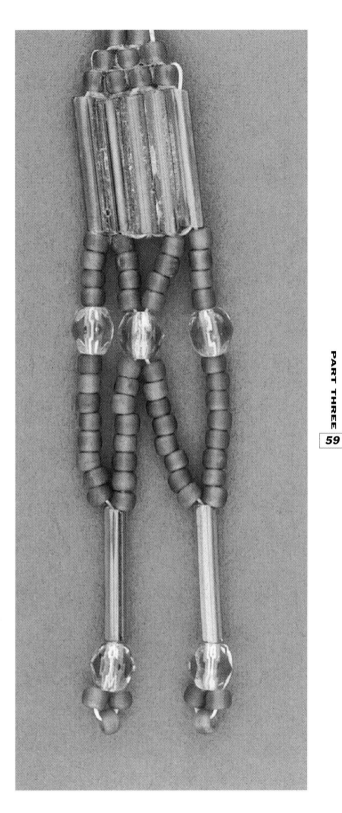

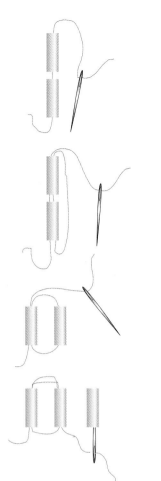

4. Be sure the netting is pulled tight, then do three rows of brick stitch.

5. To form the ear wire loop, string four beads and pass the N&T through the two top beads of the brick stitching. Reinforce by going through the loop again.

6. Weave the N&T down to the loose end and tie off.

7. Dab clear nail polish on the knot and trim.

8. Coat the BACK of the bugle row with clear nail polish to stiffen it.

9. Attach ear wires.

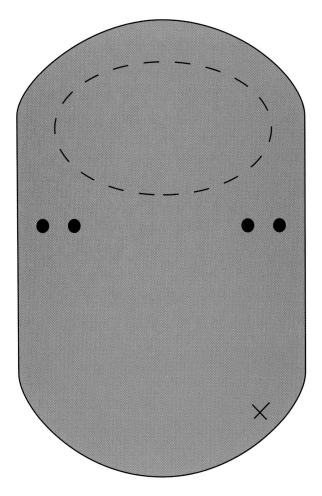

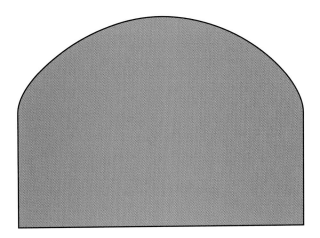

Leather Amulet Bag Template
Instructions on page 50

PART FOUR

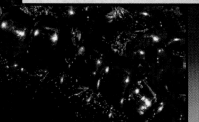

BRICK STITCH
AND
EDGE BEADING
TECHNIQUES

BRICK STITCH AND EDGE BEADING TECHNIQUES

BRICK STITCH

Due to the popularity of the triangular earrings, brick stitch is probably the most well known of the beadworking stitches. The technique produces a flexible, versatile 'bead' fabric, which upon close inspection resembles a tiny brick wall. This technique is also referred to as Commanche weave.

1. Create the start row. This is usually the widest part of the piece. The start row is most commonly done with bugle beads or one or more seed beads:

| bugle base | single-bead base | double-bead base | triple-bead base |

This stitch is also referred to as a Commanche ladder.
a. Use a single, unknotted strand of thread.
b. Pick up two beads and pull the beads to the end of the thread leaving a 4-inch tail.
c. Pass the N&T through the first bead. Holding the tail, pull the needle until the two beads are side-by-side.
e. Pass the N&T down through the second bead.
f. Pick up another bead and pass the N&T down through the second bead.
g. Pass the N&T up through the third bead.
h. Continue adding beads in this manner until the desired length is reached.
i. Reinforce the ladder by weaving back and forth through the ladder to the first bead.

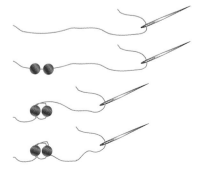

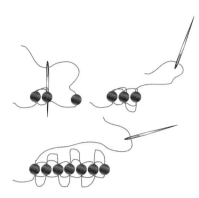

2. Do brick stitch utilizing one or both sides of the start row/Comanche ladder.
a. Pick up one bead and pass the N&T under the first loop of thread on the start row.
b. Bring the N&T through (bottom to top) the bead.
c. Continue adding beads in this manner until you have used all loops of thread on the start row.

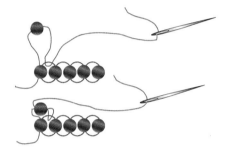

Note: brick stitch rows naturally decrease by one bead each row, thus forming a triangle.

3. To increase the number of beads in a brick stitch row, pick up two beads at the beginning of the row.

Pass the N&T under the first loop of thread and then through the SECOND picked up bead. Continue as usual across the row. At the end of the row, utilize the last loop of thread to add an additional bead.

ADDING NEW THREAD

There are two ways to add new thread. First, simply weave the old end into the beadwork, then weave in a new thread, being sure it is coming out the appropriate bead to continue brick stitching. Secondly, complete step 2a above, tie (square knot) on new thread using the old end and the new end, and do step 2b. The knot will be hidden in the bead. Weave in loose tails a bit and trim threads.

TROUBLE-SHOOTING

1. Start row is uneven -- Keep beads pulled snug together and do step 1i to snug up the beads
2. Beads sit at an angle on the start row -- Step 2b was not done
3. Threads show at the end of every other row (This is normal for traditional brick stitch).-- This is

useful in that increase beads can be attached using the end threads. Use markers to color the threads the same color as the end beads. Note: there is a weaving technique, much like increasing at the beginning of a row, that helps avoid end threads; I don't often use it because it causes the beads to sit at an odd angle.

4. **The beadwork curls** -- The tension is too loose or too tight OR the thread is too fine for the bead holes. Help avoid this by coating the back with clear nail polish and dry overnight.

EDGE BEADING

Just as the name implies, edge beading is used to finish off the edge of a piece of beadwork, especially if the bead-work is done on some kind of fabric. It may surprise some people to find edge beading lumped in with the brick stitch. Some of my students realized before I did, that simple edge beading is like brick stitch, except that the edge of the beadwork serves as the start row/Commanche ladder.

Years ago I created a kind of shorthand to help me (and eventually my students) remember how many beads to add each time. Here's an example: (3-2-2-1). The first number (3) indicates how many beads to pick up to start the edge beading. The middle numbers (2-2) indicate how many beads to add repeatedly around the beadwork. If the middle numbers are not identical, a unique pattern is being done. The last number (1) indi-cates how many beads are needed to finish off the bead-work. Although many of the projects suggest the simple 3-2-2-1 edge, there are many other possibilities. I have included some of those in this section. Feel free to make substitutions!

1. Always use **D** thread and a 10 or 12 needle for edge beading. The thicker thread fills the holes of the beads and the edge "stands up" better. Use a single, knotted strand of thread.

2. Push the N&T from the back side of the leather to the front side. This will hide the knot between the felt and leather layers. Take a tiny stitch through the leather and felt to the front edge of the beadwork. The needle should be flush against the last row of beads. If dangles will be added off the edge beading, always start the edge beading about where one of the outer dangles will begin.

3. String the indicated number of beads to start the edge, take a stitch through the edge (back to front), and pass the N&T through the last strung bead. Give a slight tug on the thread. Always take an adequate "bite" out of the fabric edge. The needle should be flush against the last bead row while

taking the stitch. Be careful not to catch any threads that hold the last bead row to the fabric.

4. Continue as in step 3, except pick up the number of beads as indicated by the middle numbers of the shorthand.

5. At the end, pick up beads as indicated by the last shorthand number.

Pass the N&T down through (top to bottom) the VERY FIRST bead in the edge, then through the felt/leather layers.

Pass the N&T back through the FIRST bead (bottom to top).

6. Weave into the beadwork and tie off OR add dangles. Push knot between felt/ leather layers to hide.

ADDING NEW THREAD

I do NOT recommend that a new thread be added. Start with enough to do the entire edge and even the dangles, if applicable.

TROUBLE-SHOOTING

1. **The first stitch is limp compared to the others.** -- It should be so, that is, until the last bead(s) is added.

2. **The spacing between the high points of the edge is uneven.** -- Practice, practice, practice. After awhile, even spacing comes naturally!

3. **The edge beading does not sit on the edge.** -- Same problem as with the brick stitch, note step 2b of brick stitch.

4. **The edge beading is loose.** -- Always give a little tug after each addition of beads.

MORE SUGGESTIONS
FOR EDGE BEADING

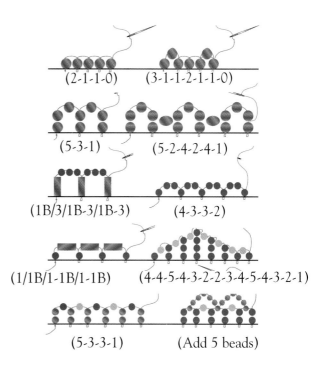

(2-1-1-0)   (3-1-1-2-1-1-0)

(5-3-1)   (5-2-4-2-4-1)

(1B/3/1B-3/1B-3)   (4-3-3-2)

(1/1B/1-1B/1-1B)   (4-4-5-4-3-2-2-3-4-5-4-3-2-1)

(5-3-3-1)   (Add 5 beads)

WILDFLOWER SET

NOTE: This technique looks best when using uniformly sized/shaped beads. Avoid using really fat, thin, or odd-shaped beads!

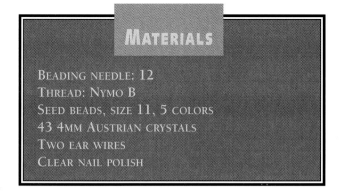

MATERIALS

BEADING NEEDLE: 12
THREAD: NYMO B
SEED BEADS, SIZE 11, 5 COLORS
43 4MM AUSTRIAN CRYSTALS
TWO EAR WIRES
CLEAR NAIL POLISH

PART I: NECKLACE

1. Start row: Leaving a 3-inch tail and using an unknotted, single strand of thread, start with a double-bead row, as illustrated below. Be sure to follow the color pattern.

2. Brick stitch single-bead rows, as illustrated. Follow the color pattern.

3. Be sure the thread is coming out the single center point bead in order to create the first dangle.
String:

> 13 color **A**
> one color **C**
> one color **E**
> one color **C**
> 4mm bead
> three color **A.**

Pass the N&T through the 4mm bead, the remaining beads, and through the center point bead.

4. Weave the N&T to the next dangle point and make another dangle. Note that each dangle decreases in length by one color **A** bead. Be sure to note the locations of each dangle and continue making dangles up one side of the pendant.

5. Weave the N&T so it is coming out the outermost bead at the top of the triangle.
String:

> two color **B**
> two color **C**
> two color **B** beads.

Pass the N&T through the second-to-last set in the double-bead row. Then pass the N&T through the outermost set and through the two **B** and the two **C** beads.

6. String six color **C** beads. Pass the N&Tthrough one color **C** bead, as illustrated.

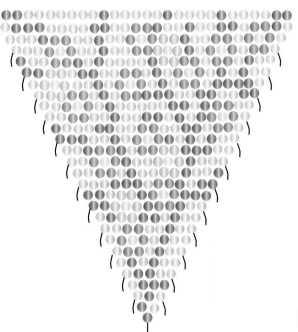

7. String one color **D** bead and pass the N&T through color **C** bead #6 toward bead #7.

8. String:

two color **B**
two color **C**
two color **B** beads.

Pass the N&T through color C beads #5 and #6 and through the two color **B** and color **C** beads, as illustrated.

9. Repeat steps 6, 7, and 8 until the flower chain is about 25 inches long. If desired, do four color **C** flowers to every one color **E** flower. Be sure to keep the beads in the chain pulled tight.

10. Attach the flower chain to the top of the other side of the pendant by stringing two color **B** beads, then passing the N&T through the appropriate double-bead set at the top edge. String two color **B** beads and pass the N&T through the other double-bead set.

Be sure the chain is NOT TWISTED!

11. Weave the N&T to the first dangle point and add dangles down the side. Note that the dangle length will increase by one color **A** bead.

12. Weave loose ends into the beadwork to secure and trim threads.

13. If desired, coat the back of the pendant with clear nail polish and allow to dry thoroughly on a flat surface. Be sure to check for colorfastness.

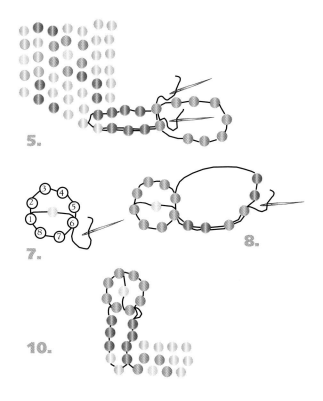

Part II: Earrings

1. Start row: double-bead row. Follow the color pattern.

2. Brick stitch single bead rows, as illustrated.

3. Make dangles up one side.

4. Weave the N&T to the fifth set of beads in the double-bead row.

String five color **A** beads, pass the N&T through the seventh double-bead set. Weave back through the fifth, the five beads and the seventh double-bead set to reinforce.

5. Make dangles down the other side.

6. Weave in loose ends and trim thread. Coat the back with clear nail polish, if desired.

7. Attach ear wires.

DONUT SET

MATERIALS

MATERIALS
NYMO THREAD: B
NEEDLES: SIZE 12
THREE 30MM GEMSTONE DONUTS
DELICA BEADS, TWO COLORS
54 6MM GEMSTONE BEADS
TWO BEAD TIPS
ONE BARREL CLASP
TWO EARRING WIRES
CLEAR NAIL POLISH

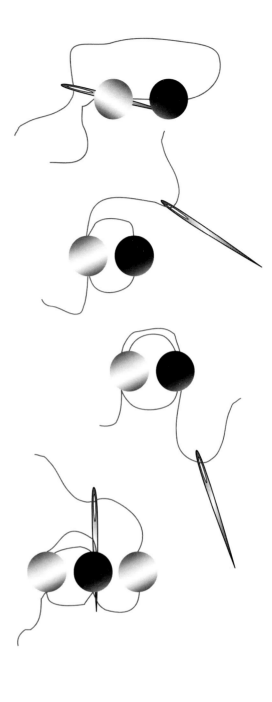

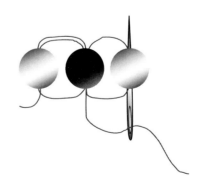

1. Use a single, unknotted strand of thread and string one **A** and one **B** Delica beads. Leaving a 3-inch tail, bring the N&T through the one **A** bead.

2. Pull the N&T until the two beads are side-by-side. Be sure to hold the thread tail!

3. Bring the N&T through the second (one **B**) bead.

4. String another 1A bead and pass the N&T through the second (one **B**) bead again.

5. Bring the N&T back through the third (one **A**) bead.

6. Continue adding beads in this manner until the entire start row is finished. Be sure to follow the pattern.

7. Reinforce the start row by passing the N&T back and forth through all the beads.

8. Pick up one **A** bead and pass the N&T under the first loop of thread on the start row.

9. Bring the N&T through the bead just picked up.

10. Pick up a one **B** bead, pass the N&T under the next loop of thread, and through the one **B** bead.

11. Continue adding beads in this manner, row by row, until the top row consists of just three beads. Each row will decrease by one bead.

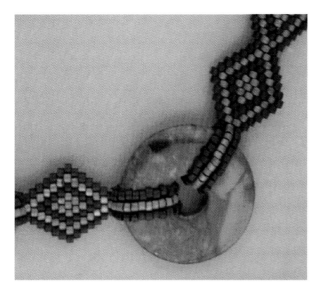

12. String 24 **A** beads, pass the N&T through the donut hole, and back through the first **A** bead.

Weave the N&T to the **B** bead, string 24 **B** beads, go through the donut hole, and back through the **B** bead. Repeat this step for the remaining **A** bead.

13. Weave the N&T back to the first bead of the start row. Turn the beadwork upside down and continue the brick stitch (instruction numbers 8-11). Be sure to follow the pattern.

14. Repeat step 12 to attach the beadwork to a second donut. Weave thread into the beadwork and trim.

15. Repeat instructions numbered 1-12 and attach the beadwork to the opposite side of the first donut.

16. Repeat step 13 and attach the beadwork (step 12) to the third donut.

17. Repeat instructions number 1-12 and attach the beadwork to the opposite side of the third donut.

18. Repeat step 13.

19. Increase EACH OF THE NEXT SIX ROWS: pick up 1A and 1B bead at the beginning of the row and pass the N&T under the first loop of thread and then through the 1B bead.

20. Continue brick stitching across the row as usual.

21. At the end of the row, stitch two beads utilizing the last loop of thread.

22. Do six rows of regular brick stitch. Be sure to follow the pattern.

23. Weave the N&T so it's coming out the center **B** bead. Remove the needle from the thread.

24. Repeat instruction numbers 17-23, but attach to the opposite side of the second donut.

25. Repeat instruction numbers 1-11, 13, 19-22 and make TWO pieces of beadwork. Weave thread into beadwork and trim.

26. Put the needle back on the donut thread and string three to six 6mm beads.

Weave the N&T through one of the beadwork pieces. The thread should exit the center **B** bead.

String eighteen to twenty one 6mm beads.

String one bead tip and a small bead.

Pass the N&T back through the hole in the bead tip and through the 6mm beads. Be sure it is tight and there is no thread showing between the beads. Weave the N&T through the beadwork again and pass the N&T through the 6mm beads again.

Weave the N&T into the beadwork attached to a donut and exit through the center B bead.

27. Repeat step 26 one or more times to reinforce.

28. Repeat steps 26-27 or the other side of the necklace.

29. Close the bead tips and attach the barrel clasp.

EARRINGS

1. Repeat steps 1-11, EXCEPT that the top row should consist of two **A** beads.

2. String six **A** beads and pass the N&T through the other **A** bead in the top row. Reinforce this loop.

3. Repeat step 13.

4. Make the dangles: string 6A beads, 6mm bead, and 3B beads.

Pass the N&T through the 6mm bead and the six **A** beads.

Pull the dangle taut and weave to the center **B** bead to make the next dangle. Each dangle increases in length by six Delica beads.

5. Weave the thread into the beadwork and trim.

6. Repeat the above steps For the second earring.

7. Attach earring wires.

8. If desired, coat the back of the beadwork with clear nail polish. This will stiffen it and secure the thread ends. Test for colorfastness!!

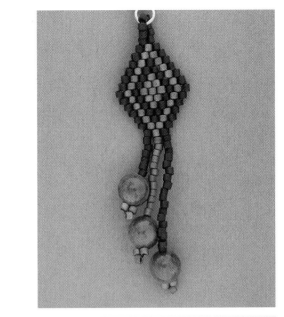

LEATHER AMULET BAG AND EARRINGS

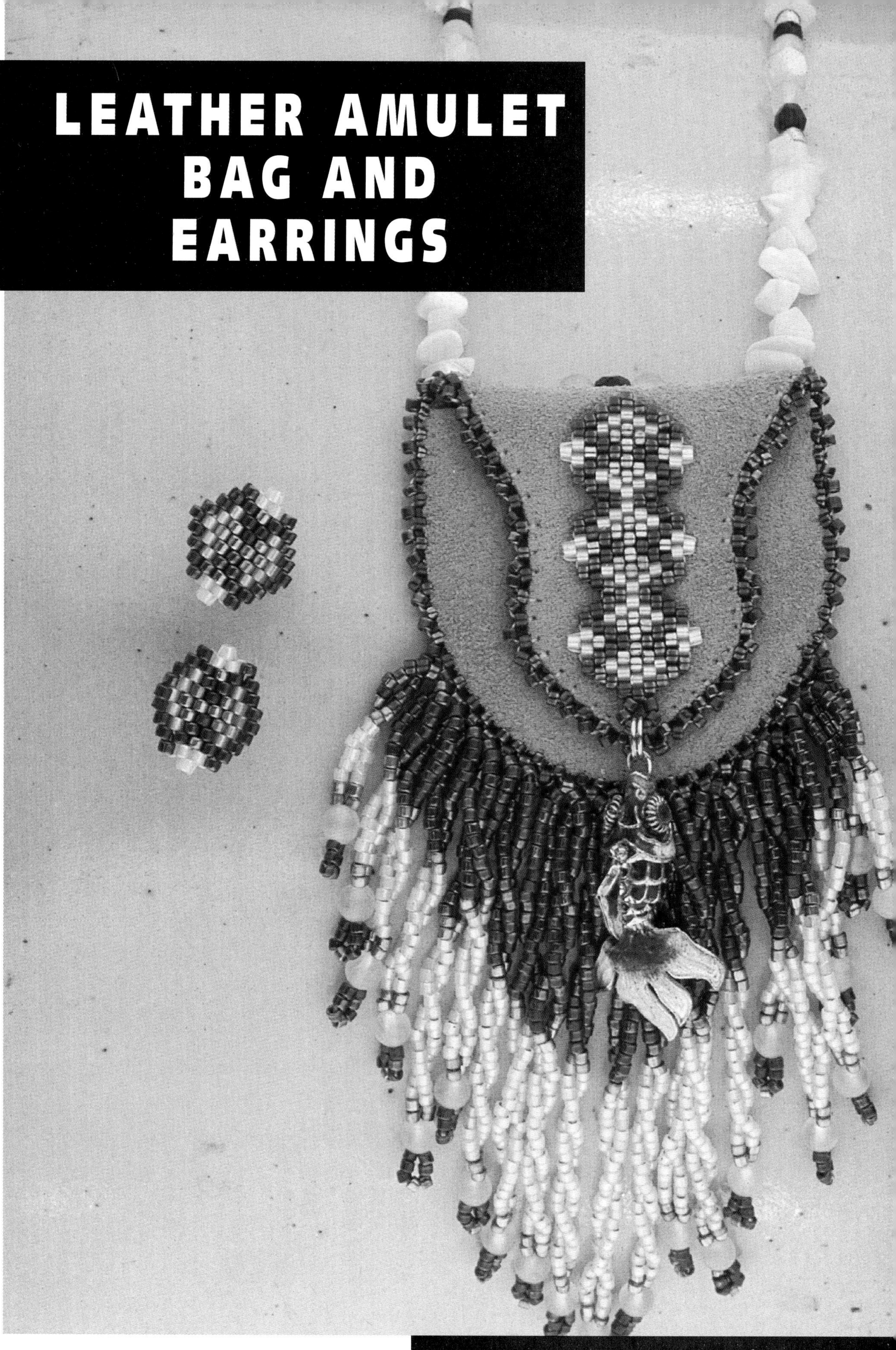

MATERIALS

Nymo™ thread, B & D
Needles, size 10 or 12
Lightweight leather scrap
One cloisonne fish or other accent
    bead (Hint: choose this first to
    determine other colors)
Delica™ beads, three colors
Stone and/or metal accent beads: chips,
    4mm round, 5mm round, etc.
Soft flex wire, 1 yard
Two crimp beads
One necklace clasp
Two ear posts
Bond 527™ glue

PART I: AMULET BAG

1. Trace the pattern on the leather scrap. Cut out the pattern pieces.

2. Use a single, unknotted strand of thread. Leave a 10-inch tail. Create the start row of the beadwork.

Add beads as illustrated until the length of 20 beads is reached. Note the color pattern!

3. Reinforce the strip, by weaving back and forth through the piece, to the first bead.

4. Do brick stitch on both sides of the start row. Carefully note the color pattern.

5. Put a needle on the 10-inch tail.

String: three Delicas, the fish (or accent) bead and three more Delicas.

Pass the N & T through the opposite side of the Delica bead on the beadwork point.

Reinforce several times. Weave into the beadwork and trim.

6. Attach the beadwork to the leather -- Attach the beadwork to the flap of the bag by using a small amount of glue and stitches.

7. Stitch the bag together -- To form the bag, position the small piece of leather over the larger. Use **D** thread and begin 3-2-1 edge beading at the **X**.

Use the edge beading to stitch the two pieces together, as well as make the decorative edge.

8. Count the number of spaces between beads on the edge, from the **X** to the same point on the other side. This will determine the number of dangles.

9. String the dangles between the points of the edge. String:

    six **A**
    two **B**
    six **C**
    two **B** (continued on next page)

4mm
three **C**
one **B**
three **C.**
Pass the N&T through the 4mm.
String:
two **B**
six **C**
two **B**
six **A.**
Pass the N&T through the next point on the edge.
Note: Each dangle increases (or decreases) by two **A** *and two* **C**.

If twisted dangles are preferable, roll the thread between the middle finger and thumb until the desired number of twists are formed. Hold the twists as the N&T passes through the edge point.

10. For the necklace chain, poke four holes in the leather. Note the two marks on the pattern and two located next to the edge beading.

Thread one end of the soft flex wire down through the hole near the edge, then up through the next hole.

String beads (length to next hole).

Pass the wire down through the third hole and up through the last hole near the edge.

11. String beads on the soft flex wire (pattern - - your choice).

String a crimping bead and the necklace clasp.

Pass the wire back through the crimping bead and, if possible, a couple of other beads.

Close the crimping bead with crimping pliers. Repeat for the other side.

12. If desired, on the back side of the flap, glue a small strip of leather over the wire.

Part II: Earrings

1. Brick stitch one segment of the flap pattern. Weave in loose threads.

2. Glue the earring post to the center back of the beadwork segment. Allow to dry for 24 hours.

3. Repeat for the other earring.

Leather template referenced in #1, page 75.

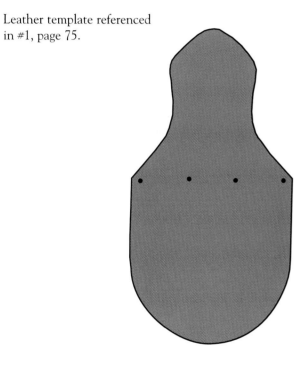

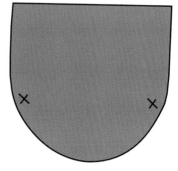

BEZELED CABOCHON SET

MATERIALS

One 30 x 40mm cabochon
Two 15 x 20mm cabochons
24 12mm oval gemstone beads
49 5mm oval silver beads
Ten 12mm oval silver filigree beads
Seed beads, size 14 (Japanese), 2 colors
Seed beads, size 11, silver-lined gray
Thread: Nymo B and D
Needles: 10 and 13
Thin leather scrap
Tiger tail or soft flex wire, 30 inches
Bond 527 glue
Two crimping beads
Necklace clasp
Two ear posts

PART I: NECKLACE

1. Use Bond 527 to glue each cabochon to a small piece of leather. Allow to dry.

2. Use a single, unknotted strand of **B** thread and string two **A** beads.

Leaving a 4-inch tail, bring the N&T through the first bead.

Pull the N&T until the two beads are next to each other.

Pass the N&T through the second bead.

String another A bead and pass the N&T through the second bead again.

Bring the N&T back through the third bead.

3. Continue adding **A** beads in this manner until the strip of beads is 68 beads long (or long enough to go around the outside edge of the cabochon; must be an even number).

4. Connect the two ends of the bead strip and place the strip around the cabochon. The thread loops should be up. Tack the bead strip down around the cabochon.

5. Bring the N&T through a bead to the front side. Do a row of brick stitch. For example, pick up one bead with the N&T and pass the N&T under the first loop of thread.

Bring the N&T through the bead just picked up.

Connect the first and last bead of the row.

6. Do a row of 4-3-3-2 edge beading.

Pick up four beads to start, skip the first loop of thread, pass the N&T under the next loop of thread, and then through the fourth bead.

Continue by picking up three beads, passing the N&T under every second loop of thread, and back through the third bead.

At the end of the row, pick up two beads and pass the N&T through the FIRST bead of the row.

Catch a thread, then pass back through the first bead.

7. Gather the beads around the cabochon by running the N&T through all the points of the edged row. Pull tight. Bring the N&T to the back, knot and trim.

8. Carefully cut out the cabochon. Leave a scant 1/16 edge; don't cut the threads!

9. Cut an oval of leather the same size as the cabochon.

Fold the tiger tail (soft flex wire) in half.

Smear the back side of the cabochon with glue. Center the tiger tail in the glue, then cover with the leather oval. Allow to dry.

10. Mark the location of the dangles.

Using **D** thread and a 10 needle, start at one point and do 1-1-1 edge beading around the cabochon to the second mark for the dangles.

While working the 1-1-1 edge beading, tug after each bead addition to pull the bead to the top. The beads should be on the top edge of the leather close to the beadwork around the cabochon.

11. Do 3-2-2-1 edge beading where the dangles will be located.

Connect the two edges, then string the dangles.
Bring the N&T out the first point of the 3-2-2-1 edge.
String:

     seven **A**
     one **C**
     seven **B**
     one **C**
     one oval
     one **C**
     four **B**
     one **C**
     four **B.**

Pass the N&T through:

     one **C**
     one oval
     one **C.**

String:

     seven **B**
     one **C**
     seven **A.**

Pass the N&T through the next point. Note that each dangle increases (or decreases) by two **A** and two **B** beads. If twisted dangles are desired, roll the thread between the middle finger and thumb until the desired number of twists are formed. Hold the twists and pass the N&T through the next point on the edge.

12. Work a row of brick stitch on the 1-1-1 edge beading. The completed bezel should curve up toward the cabochon. Tie off, trim thread and hide knot.

13. String the tiger tail with:
> one silver oval
> one gemstone oval
> one silver oval
> one gemstone oval
> one silver oval
> one silver filigree.

Repeat the above pattern five times, then string:
> one silver oval
> one gemstone
> one silver oval
> one gemstone
> one silver oval
> one crimping bead
> necklace clasp.

Pass the tiger tail back through the crimping bead and through several beads. Pull tight and close the crimping bead. Trim the excess tiger tail. Repeat for the other side.

PART II: EARRINGS

1. Repeat steps 2, 3 and 4 EXCEPT make a strip of 32 beads.

2. Do 4-3-3-2 edge beading as in step 6.

3. Do steps 7 and 8.

4. Cut a leather oval the same size as the cabochon.
Sandwich an ear post between the cabochon and the leather backing with glue. Allow to dry.

5. Do 1-1-1 edging around the cabochon as in step 10.

6. Work a row of brick stitch on the edging.
Bring N&T to back, tie off and hide knot.

7. If desired, add dangles to the earrings.
See step 11.

PEARL AND CABOCHON
NECKLACE AND
EARRINGS

MATERIALS

NYMO™ THREAD, B & D
NEEDLES, SIZE 10 & 12
ONE 25 X 30MM CABOCHON
TWO 15 X 20MM CABOCHONS
SEED BEADS, SIZE 14, ONE COLOR
ONE STRING OF FRESH-WATER PEARLS
FELT SQUARE, 4 X 4-INCH
THIN LEATHER SCRAP
SOFT FLEX WIRE, 1 YARD
BOND 527™ GLUE
TWO CRIMPING BEADS
NECKLACE CLASP
TWO EAR POSTS

PART I: NECKLACE

1. Use Bond 527™ to glue the larger cabochon to the felt. Allow to dry.

2. Use a single, unknotted strand of **B** thread. String two seed beads. Leave a 4-inch tail.

Bring the N&T through the first bead. Pull the N&T until the two beads are next to each other.

Pass the N&T through the second bead.

String another seed bead and again pass the N&T through the second bead.

Bring the N&T back through the third bead.

3. Continue adding beads in the above manner until the strip of beads is long enough to go around the outside edge of the cabochon. *Note: This must be an even number.*

4. Connect the two ends of the bead strip and place the strip around the cabochon. The thread loops should be up. Tack the bead strip down around the cabochon.

5. Bring the N&T through a bead to the front side. Do a row of brick stitch.

For example, pick up one bead with the N&T and pass the N&T under the first loop of thread. Bring the N&T through the bead just picked up. At the end of the row, connect the first and last bead.

6. Create a row of 4-3-3—2 edge beading: Pick up four beads to start, skip the first loop of thread, N&T under the second loop of thread, then through the fourth bead.

Continue by picking up three beads, passing the N&T under every second loop of thread and back through the third bead.

At the end of the row, pick up two beads and pass

the N&T through the first bead of the row, catch a thread and continue back through the first bead.

7. Gather the beads around the cabochon by running the N&T through all the points of the edged row. Pull tight. Bring the N&T through the beads to the back.

8. Create a row of back stitching around the entire cabochon and "encircle" the row.

Note: This will even out the row and reinforce the beadwork.

9. Measure the cabochon and mark the location for the center pearls.

Sew a pearl next to the row of back stitching.

Use back stitch to outline the pearl on the remaining three sides.

10. Continue adding and outlining pearls in this manner until finishing all eight.

11. Fill in the remaining exposed felt with rows of back stitching.

Don't crowd; it should be flat, not bumpy.

12. Leave a 1/16-inch edge. Carefully cut out the beadwork.

13. Fold the soft flex wire in half. Center the wire on the back and baste into place.

14. Glue the beadwork to a piece of leather. Dry thoroughly on a flat surface and trim the leather.

15. Mark the location of the dangles. Use **D** thread and a size 10 needle. Begin at one point and do 1-1—1 edge beading around the cabochon to the second mark for the dangles. As the 1-1—1 edge beading is done, tug the thread after each bead addition. This pulls the bead to the top. That is, the beads should be on the top edge of the leather close to the beadwork around the cabochon.

16. Work 3-2-2—1 edge beading where the dangles will be located. Connect the two edges, then string the dangles.

Bring the N&T out the first point of the 3-2-2—1 edge.

String 25 beads, pearl and 11 beads.

Pass the N&T through the pearl and string 25 beads.

Pass the N&T through the next edge point.

Note: Each dangle increases (or decreases) by five beads.

17. To complete the 1-1—1 edging, work a row of brick stitch. Tie off, trim thread and hide knot.

18. String the soft flex wire with a combination of beads and pearls. Complete with the crimp bead and the clasp. Pass the wire back through the crimping bead and close with pliers. Trim excess wire.

Part II: Earrings

1. Use fewer beads and repeat steps 2, 3 and 4 on previous page.

2. Work 4-3-3—2 edge beading as in step 6 on previous page.

3. Work step 7 above and carefully cut out the beadwork. Leave 1/16-inch edge.

Cut a leather oval the same size as the beadwork. Use glue and position an ear post between the cabochon and the leather backing.

Allow glue to dry.

4. Create 1-1—1 edging around the cabochon.

5. Work a row of brick stitch on the edging. Bring the N & T to the back, tie off and hide knot.

6. Repeat for the other earring.

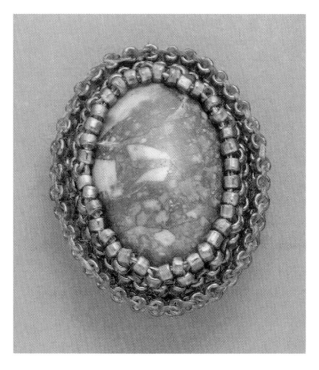

PART FIVE

PEYOTE STITCH TECHNIQUES

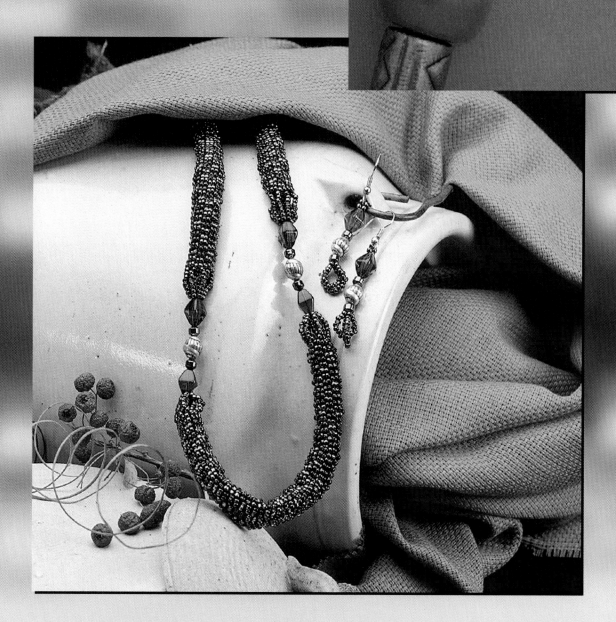

PEYOTE STITCH TECHNIQUES

Peyote stitch is a beadwork technique with several variations: tubular, flat and circular. The flexible "bead" fabric formed with this stitch has a twill pattern. This stitch is also referred to as gourd stitch. Both names are derivatives of the Native American custom of covering items used in their religious ceremonies.

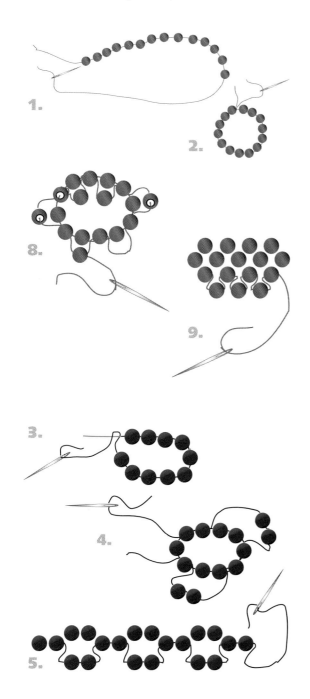

1. String the indicated number of beads.

2. Pass the N&T through all the strung beads and tie a square knot.

OR, use the loose end and the N&T end to tie a square knot.

3. Pass the N&T through the FIRST bead next to the knot.

4. String a single bead and pass the N&T through the third bead from the knot.

5. String another bead and pass the N&T through the fifth bead.

6. Continue in this manner until the entire row is complete.

7. If an UNEVEN number of beads was strung in step one, the stitch will spiral to the end.

8. If stringing an EVEN number of beads, pass the N&T through the LAST bead AND through the FIRST bead of the just completed row.

9. Fill in the spaces created by the previous row by stringing a single bead between each high bead.

10. Continue in this manner until the desired length is reached.

TWO-DROP PEYOTE

1. String an EVEN number of beads to form the base circle.

2. Pass the N&T through the first bead.

3. String two beads and pass the N&T through the 4th AND 5th beads.

4. String two more beads and pass the N&T through 8th and 9th bead.

5. Continue as above EXCEPT always string two beads and pass through two beads.

ADDING NEW THREAD

Use the end of the old thread and the end of the new thread and tie a square knot as close as possible to last bead. Put a very small dab of polish on the knot. Put a needle on each end and weave the tails into the beadwork, then trim.

TROUBLE-SHOOTING

1. Beads "pop up" instead of laying flat -- The N&T was not passed through EVERY OTHER bead, note steps 4 and 5. OR, the N&T was not passed through the first bead of the just completed row prior to starting the next row; note step 8.

2. Holes in the "bead fabric" -- High beads were skipped.

3. The pattern is off -- The beginning of each new row shifts diagonally by one bead across the pattern. Mark a diagonal line across the pattern.

ETHNIC-LOOK SET

MATERIALS

THREAD: NYMO B AND D
NEEDLES: 12
12 WOODEN OR GLASS CROW BEADS
SIX 18MM TUBULAR METAL BEADS
THREE PERUVIAN TEARDROP BEADS
20-25 PONY BEADS, SIZE 8
SEED BEADS, SIZE 11, 4 COLORS
21 INCHES OF CORD, 5/32 DIAMETER
TWO BELL CAPS
ONE BARREL CLASP
FOUR HEAD PINS

PART I: NECKLACE

1. Using a single, unknotted strand of **B** thread, string ten color **A** beads.

Leaving a 6-inch tail, tie the beads around the cord with a square knot about two inches from the middle of the cord.

2. Pass the N&T through the first bead.

3. Follow the pattern to complete the middle segment of the necklace:

      row 3: **A**
      rows 4 & 5: **B**
      rows 6 & 7: **A**
      rows 8 & 9: **C**
      rows 10 & 11: **A**
      rows 12 & 13: **B**
      rows 14 & 15: **A**
      rows 16 & 17: **D**
      rows 18 & 19: **A**
      rows 20 & 21: **B**
      rows 22 & 23: **A**
      rows 24 & 25: **C**
      rows 26 & 27: **A**
      rows 28 & 29: **B**

Then, do 35 rows of color **A** and repeat the above pattern from the bottom to the top. This measures about four inches.

4. Be sure to center the peyote stitch on the cord, then stitch through the cord and the beads a couple of times to secure. Put a needle on the loose tail and do the same.

5. String one crow, one metal, and one crow on EACH side of the tubular peyote.

6. String ten beads as in step 1 and start a new segment of tubular peyote close to the crow bead.

7. Do the peyote stitch pattern as above   rows 3-29. Then start at rows 18-19 and reverse   the pattern. The finished piece should be 2 inches long.

8. Secure both ends with stitching as in step 4.

9. Repeat steps 6-8 For the other side.

10. Repeat steps 5-9 again.

11. String one crow, one metal, and one crow on each side of the cord.

12. Put a piece of cellophane tape on each end of the cord to prevent fraying.

Cut the head off a head pin, push the pin halfway through the cord (1/4-inch from end) and twist one end of the pin around the cord several times.

Push a bell cap over the other end of the head pin.

Use round-nose pliers to form a loop in the head pin, while attaching the barrel clasp in the process. Repeat for the other side.

13. Put a knot in a single strand of **D** thread.

Push the N&T through the cord at the middle color **A** section of the tubular peyote.

Tug the thread to pull the knot into the cord.

Pass the N&T through the outermost bead of an 18-bead color **A** row.

14. String the dangles with:

> 20 **B**
>
> pony
>
> four **D**
>
> one **C**
>
> four **D** .

Pass the N&T through one and string 20 B.

Pass the N&T up through the second bead of the 18-bead row.

Weave the N&T down the third bead of the 18-bead row and string another dangle. Note that the number of color **B** beads increases (or decreases) by three beads. There should be nine dangles.

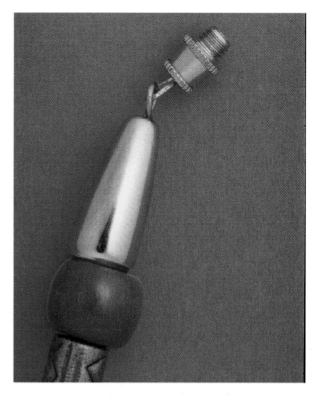

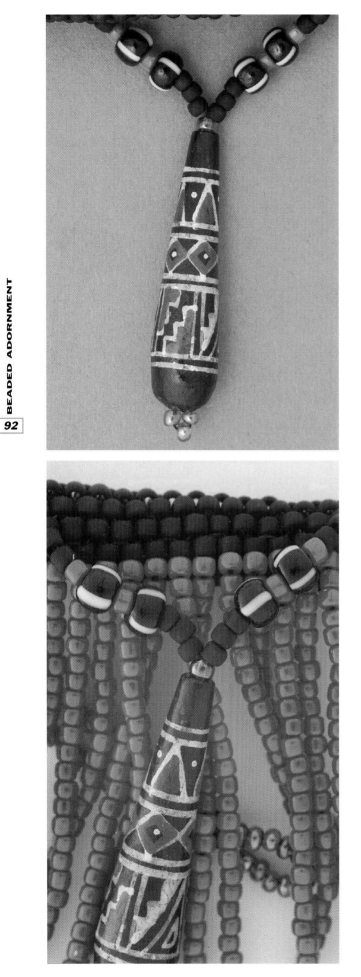

15. Weave the N&T so it's coming down out of the third bead of the 17-bead row above the 18-bead row with the dangles.

String:

> two **A**
> one **B**
> pony
> one **B**
> pony
> three **A**
> one **D**
> Peruvian
> three **D**.

Pass the N&T through the Peruvian and the one **D**. Then string:

> three **A**
> pony
> one **B**
> pony
> one **B**
> two **A**.

Pass the N&T up through the 15th bead of the 17-bead row.

16. Weave the N&T into the beadwork or cord and tie off.

PART II: EARRINGS

String a pleasing mix of pony beads and a Peruvian bead on a head pin. Use round-nose pliers to make a loop in the top. Attach ear wires. Repeat for the other earring.

LARGE-BEAD AMULET BAG SET

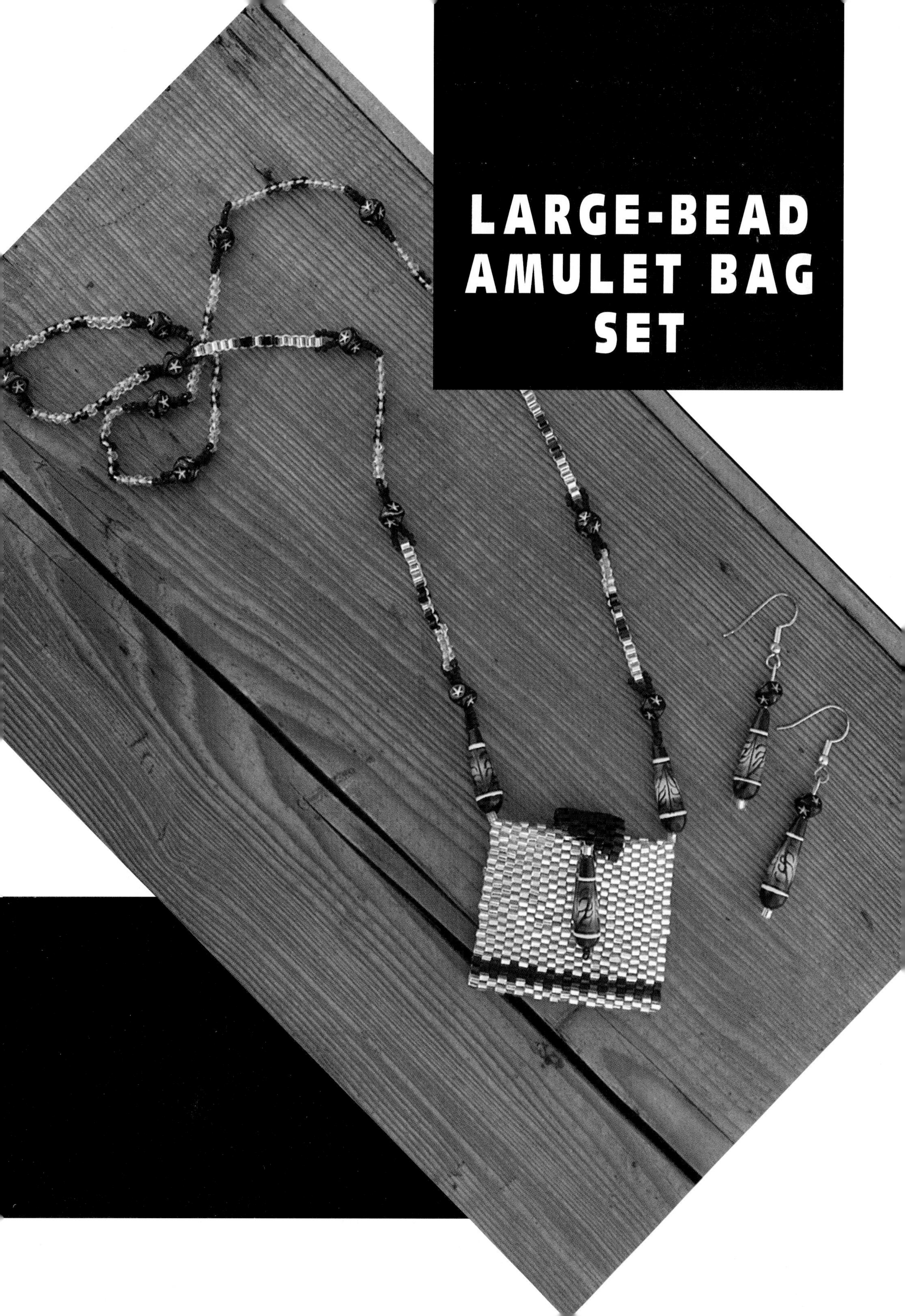

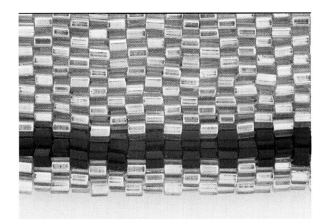

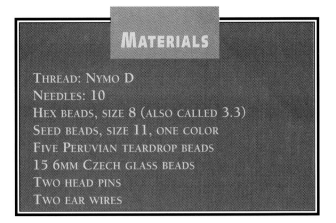

MATERIALS

THREAD: NYMO D
NEEDLES: 10
HEX BEADS, SIZE 8 (ALSO CALLED 3.3)
SEED BEADS, SIZE 11, ONE COLOR
FIVE PERUVIAN TEARDROP BEADS
15 6MM CZECH GLASS BEADS
TWO HEAD PINS
TWO EAR WIRES

PART I: AMULET BAG

1. Using a double-strand of thread, string 42 color **A** beads.

Leaving a 4-inch tail, tie a square knot to form a circle of beads.

2. If desired, place the circle of beads over the cardboard center of a toilet paper roll. If necessary, cut the cardboard roll lengthwise to make it adjustable in size.

Pass the N&T through the first bead.

3. Do 28 rows of peyote stitch with color **A** beads. Then do three rows with color **B** beads. Finally, do three rows with color **A**.

4. Carefully flatten the beadwork. Flattened the beadwork so that the bottom beads fit together like zipper teeth.

5. Sew the bottom together by passing the N&T back and forth through the beads of the last row.

6. Weave the N&T to the top back of the bag. The side of the bag with ten high beads is the back of the bag. Weave the N&T so it is coming out the fourth high bead from the side edge.

7. Do ten rows (seven beads wide) of peyote stitch. Do six rows and decreased each by one bead to form the angle. Because there is an UNEVEN number of beads, it will be necessary to do this special weave stitch at ONE END OF THE ROW to get into position to do the next row:

8. Weave the N&T so it is coming out the fourth bead of the flap. String 1A, Peruvian, and three seed beads. Pass the N&T through the Peruvian and the 1A. Pass the N&T through the OPPOSITE side of the fourth flap bead. Reinforce.

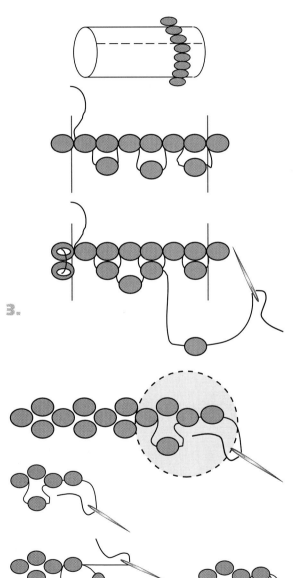

PART II: CHAIN

9. Weave the N&T so it's coming out the outermost low bead on the top back of the bag.

10. String:

> one **A**
> Peruvian
> four seed beads
> 6mm
> four seed beads.

11. Do a 15-bead Commanche ladder (5A, 2B, 1A, 2B, 5A). Be sure to pull the ladder tightly next to the strung beads.

12. String four seed beads, 6mm and four seed beads.

13. Repeat steps 11 and 12 eleven times.

14. String Peruvian and one **A**. Pass the N&T through the other outermost bead on the top back.

15. Pass the N&T through the one **A** and the Peruvian bead.

String four seed beads and pass the N&T through the 6mm bead. String four seed beads and reinforce the 15-bead ladder by passing the N&T back and forth through the beads.

16. Continue adding seed beads and reinforcing ladders until the entire chain has been done.

17. Pass the N&T through the Peruvian and one **A** bead. Weave the N&T into the amulet bag, tie off and trim thread.

PART III: EARRINGS

String one **A**, Peruvian and 6mm on a head pin. Use round-nose pliers to form a loop in the head pin. Attach ear wire. Repeat for the other earring.

TWO-DROP PEYOTE SET

MATERIALS

THREAD: NYMO B
NEEDLES: 13
SEED BEADS, SIZE 11, 3 COLORS
SIX 8MM SILVER BEADS
TEN 8MM CZECH GLASS BEADS
12 5MM GEMSTONE BEADS
ONE BARREL CLASP
TWO BEAD TIPS
TWO EAR WIRES

PART I: NECKLACE

1. String 16 color **A** beads.
Leaving a 6-inch tail, tie a square knot to form a circle of beads.

2. If desired, place the circle of beads around a straw or pencil. Pass the N&T through the first bead.

3. Using two-drop peyote stitch, do 5 3/4 inches for the middle segment of the necklace. Be sure to follow the color pattern. Tie off and leave a remaining thread.

4. Repeat steps 1, 2, and 3 to make the two side segments. Each should be 3 1/2 inches in length. Tie off, but leave remaining thread.

5. Attach the middle segment to each of the side segments with 2 1/2 inches of strung beads: tie on (or use remaining threads, if long enough) using the loose tail of the middle segment. Weave the N&T until it is coming out a pair of the high points of the peyote stitch, as illustrated.

String:

> three **A**
> two **B**
> three **A**
> 8mm
> 5mm
> silver
> 5mm
> 8mm
> three **A**
> two **B**
> three **A**.

Pass the N&T through a pair of high points on the side segment.

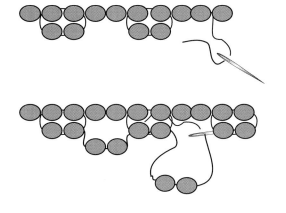

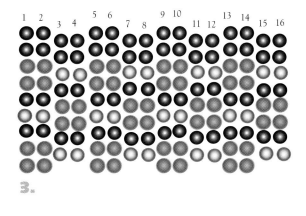

3.

6. String 3A, 2B, and 3A.

Pass the N&T through the large beads and string 3A, 2B, and 3A.

Pass the N&T through the OPPOSITE side of the original high points.

Weave the N&T to the next pair of high points and repeat. Note that only seed beads will be strung and the N&T will pass through the large beads each time. Be careful not to twist the segments and be sure to keep it pulled tight.

Tie off and weave in loose ends.

7. Attach the side segments to the barrel clasp: tie on using the loose tail of a side segment. Weave the N&T until it is coming out a pair of the high points.

String:

three **A**
two **B**
three **A**
8mm
5mm
silver
5mm
8mm
a bead tip.

String one **A** (with a large hole) and pass the N&T back through the bead tip and the large beads. Pull tight!

Continue as in step 6, except that seed beads are only strung on the peyote end and the N&T will pass through the large beads and the bead tip EACH TIME.

Tie off and weave loose ends into the beadwork.

8. Close the bead tips and attach the barrel clasp.

9. Use a single, unknotted strand of thread and string four **A** beads.

Leaving a 4-inch tail, pass the N&T through all four beads to form a loop.

10. String:

> 8mm
> 5mm
> silver
> 5mm
> three A
> two B
> six A
> two B
> three A.

Pass the N&T through the large beads, the four-bead loop, and back through the large beads.

> String:
> three **A**
> two **B**
> eight **A**
> two **B**
> three **A.**

Pass the N&T through the large beads and the four-bead loop again.

11. Use the loose tail and the N&T to tie off. Dab knot with polish and trim.

12. Repeat for the other earring.

13. Attach ear wires.

BUTTERFLY AMULET SET

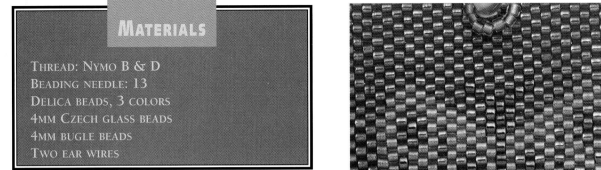

MATERIALS

THREAD: NYMO B & D
BEADING NEEDLE: 13
DELICA BEADS, 3 COLORS
4MM CZECH GLASS BEADS
4MM BUGLE BEADS
TWO EAR WIRES

PART I: AMULET BAG

1. String 84 color **A** beads. Leaving a 4-inch tail, tie a square knot to form a circle of beads.

2. If desired, place the circle of beads over a cardboard toilet paper roll. If necessary, cut the cardboard roll lengthwise to make it adjustable. Pass the N&T through the first bead.

3. Starting at the bottom, follow the pattern and do 61 rows of tubular peyote stitch. Note that the back side of the bag does NOT have the butterfly motif; therefore, only the front side of the pattern is printed. Because the first bead in each subsequent row of tubular peyote stitch shifts by one, it is helpful to color a diagonal line across the pattern. Use this pattern as the starting point for each new row.

4. Do tubular peyote stitch with color **A** beads until the bag measures 2 1/2 inches.

Remove the beadwork from the cardboard roll and carefully flatten it and center the butterfly in the front.

3.

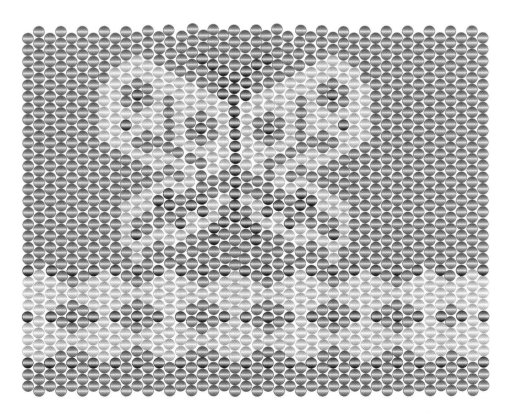

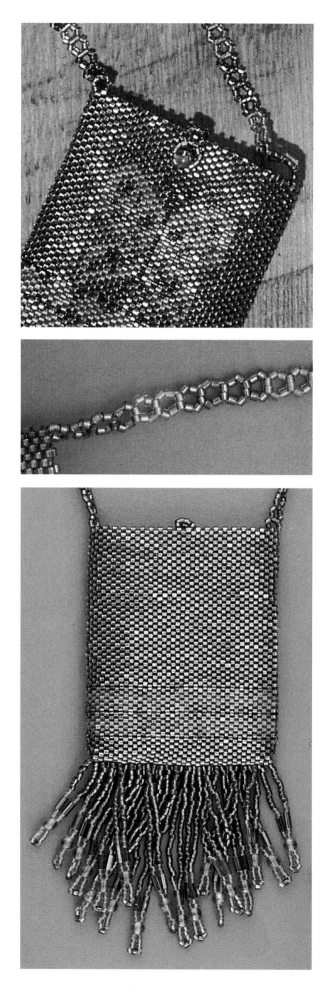

5. Top closure -- Weave the N&T so it is coming out the 11th high bead from the edge of the bag.

String six **A** and pass the N&T through the 12th high bead, the low bead and the 11th high bead again. Then pass the N&T through four strung beads.

String six **A** and pass the N&T through two beads on the first bead circle AND through four of the just strung beads.

String six **A** and repeat the preceding step.

String 11 **B** and pass the N&T through two beads on the third circle, as well as all 11 **B** beads. Weave the N&T through the bead circles to strength.

Weave the thread into the beadwork and tie off.

Sew on (as you would a button) a 4mm bead centered above the butterfly's head.

6. Chain -- Add enough new **D** thread to do the entire chain. Utilizing a high-low-high bead on the side of the bag, make the first bead circle as described and illustrated in step 5.

Continue making bead circles, until the chain is the desired length (pattern -- four color **A**, two color **B** circles).

Attach the end of the chain to high-low-high beads on the other side of the bag.

Weave the thread into the beadwork and tie off. Trim.

7. Bottom flap -- Use the loose tail to tie on new thread.

Weave the N&T so it's coming out the 20th bead from the front center line (marked with an * on the pattern).

Use color A beads and do eight rows of flat peyote stitch. Each row will be 19 beads wide.

8. Fold the bottom flap to the other side of the bag and stitch together.

Weave the N&T to the center row of the flap and add the dangles.

String:

    ten **A**
    two **B**
    bugle
    two **B**
    4mm
    four **B**
    one **A**
    four **B.**

Pass the N&T through the 4mm and string 2B, bugle, 2B, and 10A.

Pass the N&T through the next bead in the peyote row.

Continue stringing dangles, noting that each increases (or decreases by 2A beads). There should be 19 dangles.

Weave the thread into the beadwork, tie off and trim.

Part II: Earrings
(Worked with a Brick Stitch)

1. Make a single-bead Commanche ladder that is seven beads wide (pattern – one **A**, five **B**, one **A**).

2. Follow the color pattern and brick stitch the top of the earring.

3. Add a six-bead loop for the ear wire.

4. Weave down the side of the earring and string the dangles.

String:

> five **A**
> two **B**
> bugle
> two **B**
> 4mm
> four **B**
> one **A**
> four **B.**

Pass the N&T through the 4mm, two **B**, bugle, two **B**, five **A** and the first bead in the Commanche ladder.

Weave to the next bead in the Commanche ladder and string another dangle. Note that the dangles increase (or decrease) by two **A** beads.

5. Weave the loose threads into the beadwork and trim.

6. Attach an ear wire.

7. Repeat for the other earring.

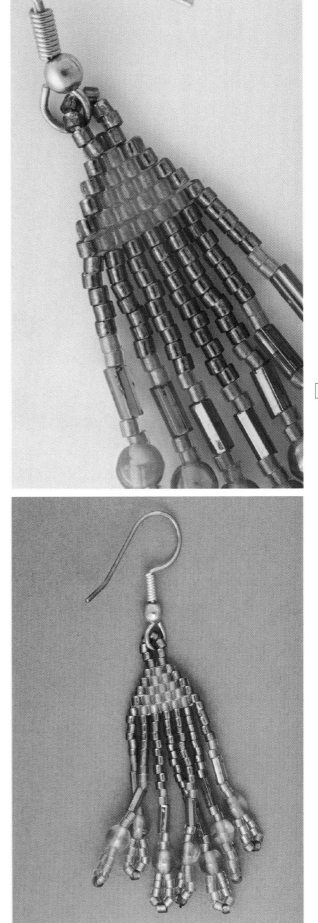

PART SIX SPLIT-LOOM TECHNIQUES

Loomwork is significantly different than the other beadwork techniques in this book. The technique requires an additional piece of equipment, the loom, and uses two sets of threads, the warp threads and the weft thread. The warp threads are more-or-less attached permanently during the looming process. Use the weft thread to weave beads between the warp threads.

There are numerous looms available, from the metal or plastic kiddie looms to $100 adult versions. Don't even waste your money on the kiddie looms; they will not work for these split-loom necklaces. In looking at other looms, there are several points to consider. First, is the loom long enough? It should be at least 25 inches long to accommodate these necklaces. Second, does the loom utilize a spring to hold the warp threads in place? Some looms use strung beads instead of the coils of the spring. The problem with this is, whenever the loom is moved, the warp threads easily "jump" the beads resulting in a tangled mess. Third, does the loom have a solid piece of wood forming the base? This provides a very handy "table" for patterns and bead trays during the looming process. Fourth, is the length of the loom adjustable? This may or may not be a good thing. Adjustable looms are often so long that they're very cumbersome and awkward to work with. Note that it is easy to get the warp threads too tight, which causes the threads to stretch and results in puckered loomwork. Finally, does the loom cost an arm and a leg and your first-born? Frankly, why spend $80-100 when you can make your own for $8-10?

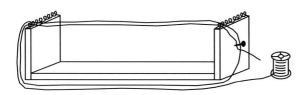

1a-f

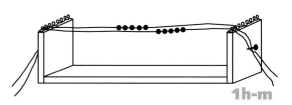

1h-m

1. Once a loom has been procured, the first step in using it is stringing the warp threads.

   a. Use **D** thread for stringing the warp threads.

   b. If you are not stringing beads on the warp threads, tie the thread onto the nail. Leave about a 10-inch tail of thread.

   c. Place the thread in a coil on the spring, then across the loom to the corresponding coil on the OPPOSITE end of the loom.

   d. Wrap the thread around the base of the loom.

   e. Place the thread in an adjacent coil and continue with steps c & d until the desired number of warp threads have been strung.

   f. Tie the thread around the nail, leaving about a 10-inch tail.

   g. Remove the completed loomwork from the loom by cutting the warp threads under the base of the loom.

   h. If stringing beads on the warp threads, note that EACH warp thread will be cut to length (usually about 40 inches for these necklaces) and tied individually to the loom.

   i. Cut the indicated number of threads.

   j. Leaving a 10-inch tail, tie one end of the first thread around the nail.

   k. Put a needle (size 10) on the other end of the thread and string the indicated number and sequence of beads.

   l. Remove the needle, place the thread in the same coil at the opposite end of the loom, and tie the thread around the nail.

m. Repeat steps i, j, and k for the remaining warp threads.

n. Remove the completed loomwork from the loom by UNTYING the knots.

o. Try to string the loom so the warp threads are reasonably taut. Don't be concerned if the threads sag a bit. Be careful about getting the warp threads too tight; this could cause puckered loomwork!

p. It's important that the above stringing techniques be used. These necklaces require a considerable amount of thread on BOTH sides of the loomwork to accommodate the dangles and tying off the neck strap. Wrapping around the nail in the stringing process, or cutting the warp threads at the nail may not allow for enough thread.

2. The next step in loomwork is weaving with the weft thread. (If the terms warp and weft are confusing, remember weft and weave both begin with the letters w-e.)

a. Use 4-6 feet of **B** thread to begin.

b. Leaving a tail, tie a loose, single knot onto the outermost warp thread. The patterns indicate how far from the end of the loom to tie on the weft thread. It is also wise to tie on at the end with the longest thread tails. Use these tails to string the dangles.

c. Thread a 12 LONG needle onto the weft thread.

d. Use a post-it-note or a ruler to mark the first row of the pattern. Read the pattern from LEFT TO RIGHT and string the indicated number and sequence of beads.

e. Slide the beads down next to the knot.

f. Bring the N&T UNDER the warp threads and push the beads UP between the warp threads. There should be ONE bead between each warp thread.

g. Pass the N&T over the top of the warp threads (including the opposite outermost) through the row of beads. Note that the first row is the most difficult. It may be easier for beginners to pass the N&T through 5-6 beads at a time, rather than trying to do the entire row at once.

h. Move the row marker and continue with the above steps, looming the entire piece.

3. A couple of the necklaces require that the width of the row be decreased.

a. Pass the N&T through the number of beads in the previous row, which you will decrease in the new row.

b. Wrap the weft thread around the outermost warp thread of the new row.

c. String the indicated number and sequence of beads and weave with the weft thread as described above. However, note that the outer most warp thread has also shifted.

4. Upon removal of the loomwork from the loom, there will be 'zillions' of warp threads that have to be dealt with in some way. Often this means weaving the warp threads into the loomed piece.

a. Put a size 10 needle on the warp thread.

b. Weave the N&T back and forth vertically through ONLY that row as indicated. Weave through six-ten beads, depending on if the thread is a weight-bearing one.

c. Pass the N&T through six-ten beads in a horizontal row and trim the thread. Keep track of which horizontal rows are used; in other words, vary them or it will soon become impossible to get a needle through the beads. This could even result in a broken bead. Heaven forbid!

ADDING NEW THREAD

The only time to do this is after weaving a row of beads. Tie on a new weft thread as in 2b above, or if knots are not desirable, weave in a new weft thread by passing the N&T through 3-4 rows. Weave the loose ends into the loomwork and trim.

TROUBLE-SHOOTING

1. **The first bead falls off** -- The weft thread did not pass over the TOP of the outermost warp thread. Pull the weft thread out of the row of beads, string a new bead and try again.

2. **The loomwork is not flat and/or some beads sag** -- The weft thread did not go over the TOP of the warp threads. If there are only a few, correct the problem when weaving in warp threads at the end. Otherwise, redo the rows.

3. **The design is off** -- Remember to always read LEFT TO RIGHT; use something to mark the rows; be careful in noting number and sequence of beads per row.

4. **Skipped an entire row** -- Believe it or not, it is possible to add a row. Carefully cut the loop of weft thread around the outermost warp thread (next to where you are adding the row). Push the loomed rows apart to make enough space to add the row. Weave in a new weft thread and take care to go several times through the row with the cut loop. Loom the new row. Weave the weft thread into the loomwork and trim.

SEE PAGE 117 FOR ILLUSTRATIONS.

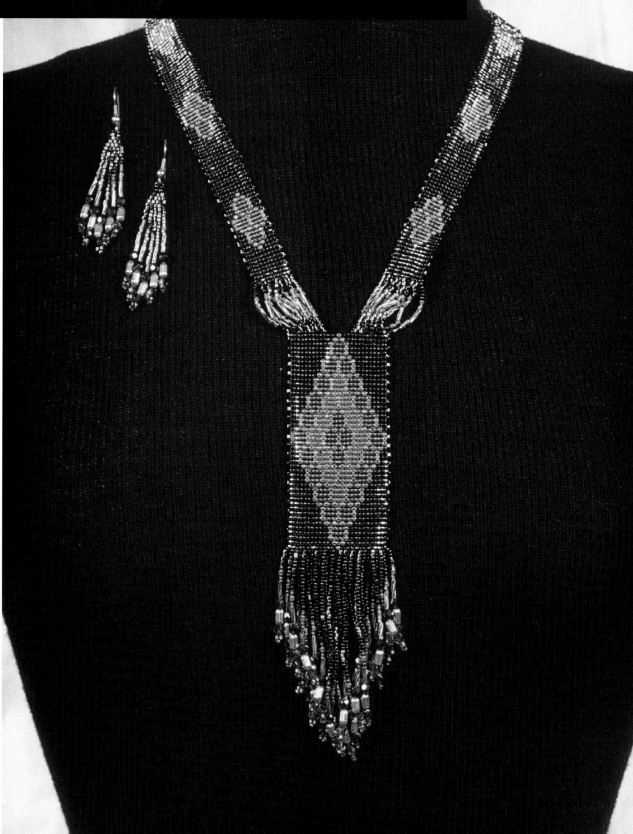

"STAINED GLASS" NECKLACE AND EARRINGS

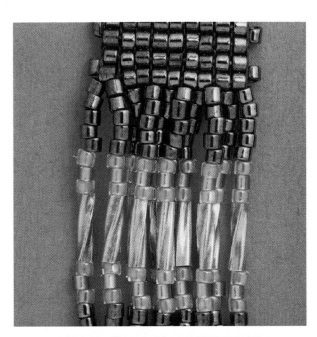

MATERIALS

BEADING LOOM, AT LEAST 25 INCHES LONG
NYMO™ THREAD, B & D
NEEDLES, 12 LONG
DELICA™ BEADS, FOUR COLORS
ACCENT BEADS: CRYSTALS, BUGLES, CZECH
      GLASS, METALLIC, ETC. (YOUR CHOICE)

PART I: NECKLACE

1. Cut 20 pieces of **D** thread, each 40 inches long. On each of the first ten threads, string:

    five **A**
    one **B**
    one **C**
    one **B**
    bugle
    one **B**
    one **C**
    one **B**
    five **A**

Tie each thread onto the loom.

2. String six threads onto the loom with no beads. (Note: there is a total of 26 threads.)

Repeat the second part of step 1 with the remaining ten threads. Push the strung beads to one side.

3. Start at the other side about four inches from the end.

Tie on **B** thread and loom the large pattern (bottom to top). After completing the piece, loosen the tie-on knot and weave the loose tail into the loomwork.

4. Push the first set of strung beads (ten threads/17 beads) next to the completed loomwork.

Tie on **B** thread and loom the small pattern (bottom to top).

Note: Repeat the pattern five times.

5. Repeat for the other side. Loom the small pattern **six times**.

6. **Edge the loomwork**: This will strengthen the necklace, hide uneven edges and give a finished appearance. Weave in **new** thread.

Bring the N&T out the bottom row of the large pendant.

String one **A** and pass the N&T through the first two beads of the **next** row.

Pass the N&T up through the same two beads on the **third** row.

String another **A** bead and repeat the process. Continue until all the loomwork has been edged.

Move to the next piece of loomwork; pass the N&T through the strung beads between the loomed pieces.

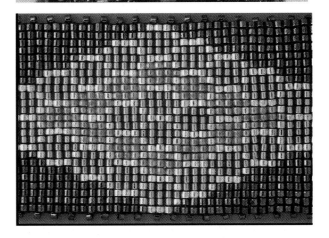

7. To remove the beadwork from the loom, **untie** the knots on the large pendant end. On the other end, cut the threads at the nail.

8. Weave the six plain threads into the loomwork and trim the threads.

9. **Attach the two ends of the neck chain** -- Put a needle on each of the outermost threads. In turn, weave each thread into the loomwork on the **opposite side**. Continue weaving all pairs of threads. Trim threads.

10. **String the dangles**: Put a needle on the outermost thread.

String:

> five **A**
> two **B**
> one **C**
> two **B**
> accent beads
> three **B.**

Pass the N&T through the accent beads, two **B**, one **C**, two **B**, five **A**.

Weave into the loomwork 1/2 to 3/4 inch. Trim thread.

Continue stringing dangles until finishing all 26. *Note: Each dangle increases (or decreases) by three **A**.*

11. *Optional: To set the knots and stiffen the beadwork, coat the back with a generous amount of clear nail polish. First test for colorfastness!*

PART II: EARRINGS
(WORKED WITH THE BRICK STITCH)

1. Leave a 4-inch tail. Create a five bead wide, single-bead Commanche ladder. Note the photograph.

2. Follow the color pattern and brick stitch three rows.

3. String four beads and form the ear wire loop as shown in photograph.

4. Weave the N & T to the first bead of the start row and string the dangles.

String:

> five **A**
>
> two **B**
>
> one **C**
>
> two **B**
>
> accent beads
>
> three **B** .

Pass the N & T through the accent beads, the seed beads and down through the second bead on the start row.

Continue stringing dangles.

*Note: The dangles increase (or decrease) by 2**A**.*

5. Weave the thread ends into the beadwork and trim.

6. Repeat for other earring.

7. *Optional: To stiffen, coat the back with clear nail polish.*

8. Attach ear wires.

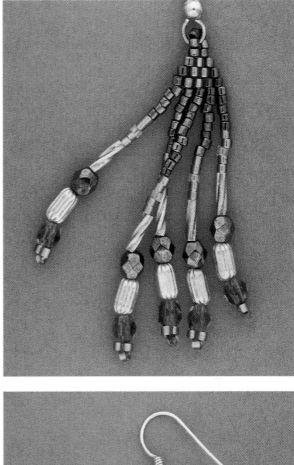

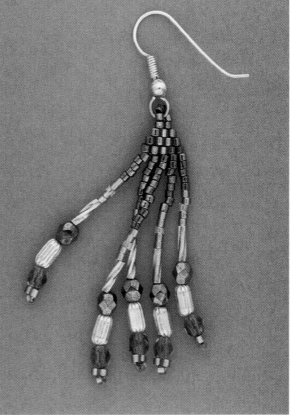

SNOWFLAKE
SET

PART I: NECKLACE

1. Warp threads: cut 39 pieces of size **D** thread that are EACH 40 inches long.

On EACH of the first 16 threads, string 150 color **A** beads.

String seven threads with no beads.

String 150 color **A** beads on each of the last 16 threads. (Attach/tie one end of the thread to the loom, put needle on the other end, string 150 beads, remove needle, and attach/tie thread to the opposite end of the loom. Threads should be reasonably taut.)

Push the beads to one side.

(30 strung beads per warp thread)

    color **A**

    silver

    white

2. Starting at the other side, about five inches from the end, tie on **B** thread and loom the large snowflake pattern (bottom to top). After completing the piece, loosen the tie-on knot and weave the loose thread tail into the loomwork, as well as the weft thread.

3. Push the first set of beads (16 threads/30 beads each) next to the completed snowflake.

Tie on **B** thread and loom (bottom to top) a small snowflake. Repeat until looming all five small snowflakes.

Weave in loose threads.

4. Repeat for the other side, except ONLY LOOM four SMALL SNOWFLAKES.

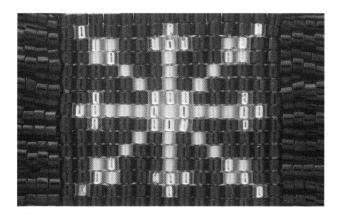

5. Edge the loomwork -- I like to do this because it strengthens the necklace, tends to hide uneven edges, and gives a finished appearance.

Weave in new thread, bringing the N&T out the bottom row of the large snowflake.

String one silver bead, and pass the N&T through the first two beads of the NEXT row.

Pass the N&T up through the same two beads on the THIRD row.

String another silver bead and repeat the process.

Continue edging until completing all the loomwork. To move from one snowflake to the next, pass the N&T through the strung beads between the loomed pieces.

6. Remove the beadwork from the loom by UNTYING the knots.

Tie a LOOSE temporary knot in each of the sides.

7. Weave the seven plain threads into the loom work and trim the threads.

8. Attach the two ends -- Put a needle on the outermost thread and pass the N&T through the beads to the loomwork.

Weave the N&T through several rows, tie a knot around a warp thread and pull the knot into the closest bead.

Weave the N&T into a couple more beads and trim the thread. Continue in this manner until all 32 threads on each side are complete.

9. String the dangles -- Put needle on the outermost thread, and string:

> three **A**
> 5mm
> bugle
> 5mm
> three **A**

Pass the N&T through the 5mm, bugle, 5mm and 3A.

Weave it into several rows of loomwork.

Knot around a warp thread, pull the knot into the closest bead, weave through a couple more beads and trim the thread. Follow the pattern, noting that the numbers indicate the number of color **A** beads strung each time, until all 39 dangles have been done.*

10. If desired, coat the back with a generous amount of clear nail polish. This sets the knots and stiffens the beadwork.

Be sure to test for colorfastness!!

*The numbers are not here to indicate how many to string for each dangle.

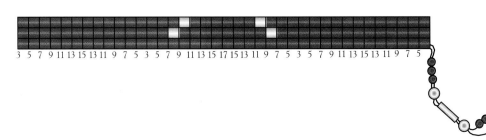

3 5 7 9 11 13 15 13 11 9 7 5 3 5 7 9 11 13 15 17 15 13 11 9 7 5 3 5 7 9 11 13 15 13 11 9 7 5

Part II: Earrings
(Worked in the Brick Stitch)

1. Leaving an 8-inch tail, make a single-bead Commanche ladder that is 17 beads wide. Note the color pattern.

2. Follow the pattern and brick stitch one side.

3. Weave the N&T down the side to the first bead of the ladder/start row.

4. Turn the beadwork over and brick stitch the other side.

5. Weave the thread into the beadwork and trim.

6. Put a needle on the 8-inch tail and string five beads.

Pass the N&T through the OPPOSITE side.

Reinforce, then weave into the beadwork and trim.

7. Attach an ear wire.

8. Repeat for the other earring.

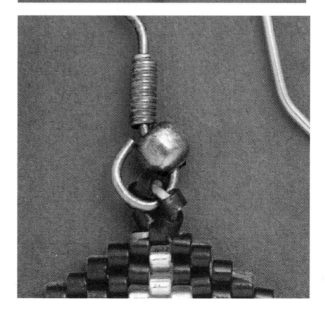

GEOMETRIC
BUGLE SET

PART I: NECKLACE

1. Measure your bugle beads in comparison to the Delica beads; number of Delicas equal one bugle. These directions presume that five Delicas equal one bugle.

2. String the loom with D thread: tie on, string five warp threads, skip five coils on the loom, string 18 threads, skip five coils again, and string five warp threads. There should be 28 total warp threads.

Determine the number of coils to skip by comparing the length of the bugle in comparison to the Delicas (step 1).

3. Leaving a 30-inch tail, tie on **B** thread about 8 inches from one end. Starting at the arrow, follow the pattern and loom (bottom to top) the square part of the pendant.

4. To do the point at the top, pass the N&T UNDER the outermost warp thread. Back through the beads in the last row until the N&T is at the first (*) warp thread of the shorter row. Loop the weft under and then over this outermost warp thread. String the beads for the shorter row and bring them under the warp threads and proceed as usual. Repeat for the other rows. Bring the N&T back into the loomwork and tie off. Trim thread.

5. Put a needle on the 30-inch tail at the bottom of the loomwork. Decreasing, add the bottom seven rows.

Weave the N&T back into the loomwork and tie off. Trim thread.

6. Attach a weft thread to the upper right and loom the neck chain. When completed, it should be about 13 inches long.

7. Reinforce the necklace by edging the outermost edge.

String one **C** bead and pass the N&T through two rows, string another **C** bead, and pass the N&T through two rows, etc.

Edge the ENTIRE right side.

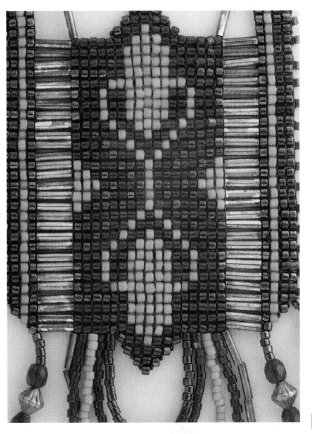

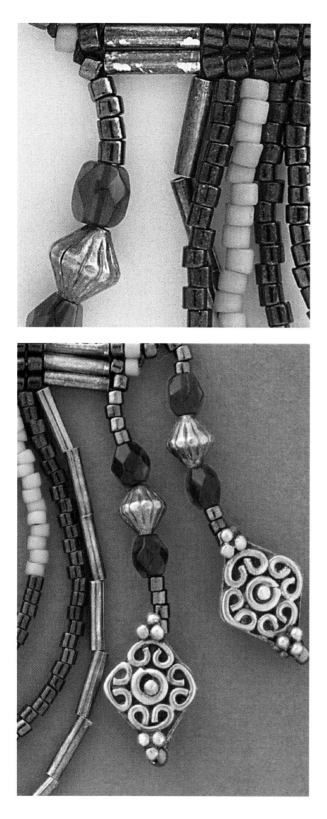

8. Repeat steps 6 and 7 for the left side of the neck chain.

9. Weave loose ends into the loomwork and trim.

10. Remove the loomwork from the loom by cutting the warp threads close to the nails.

11. Connect the two ends of the neck chain by weaving each of the five threads on each side into the OPPOSITE side.

12. Except for one outermost thread on EACH side, weave the warp threads at the top of the pendant into the loomwork. Trim.

13. String:

> five bugles
> one 4mm glass
> one 4mm silver
> one 4mm glass

Repeat this sequence, to reach the desired length, on the remaining threads. It should be the same length as the loomed chain. If the threads are long enough, weave the ends into the loomwork and tie off. If they're too short, tie the two ends together and hide knots. Trim threads.

14. Note which of the warp threads at the bottom of the pendant will be used for dangles. Weave the remainder into the loomwork. Trim threads.

15. String the two outermost dangles on each side. String:

> three **A**
> one 4mm glass
> one 4mm silver
> one 4mm glass
> three **A**
> Thai-silver
> one **A**.

Pass the N&T back through the Thai-silver, 3A, 4mm, and 3A.

Weave the thread into the loomwork and trim thread. Note that the length of the longer dangles increases to four **A**.

16. String the loop dangles. Begin with the shortest thread and string 15 Delicas, one 4mm silver and 15 Delicas.

Weave the end into the loomwork.

Pass the other warp thread through the bead loop and weave the end into the loomwork. Trim thread. Note that the number of Delicas strung on EACH side of the 4mm increases by five beads.

String the following to form the largest loop:

> seven bugles
> one 4mm glass
> one 4mm silver
> one 4mm glass
> seven bugles

17. Coat the back side of the pendant with clear nail polish to set the knots and stiffen the loomwork. Test for colorfastness!

PART II: EARRINGS

String:
   Thai-silver
   4mm glass
   4mm silver
   4mm glass on a head pin.
Use round-nose pliers to form a loop in the head pin. Attach ear wire. Repeat for the other earring.

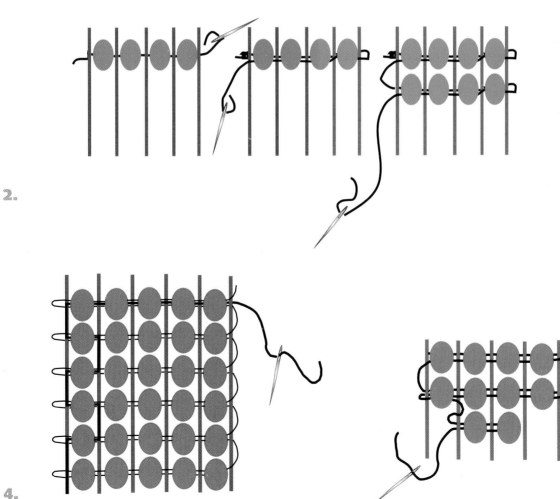

2.

4.

3.

PART SEVEN
GALLERY OF BEADWORK BY ALASKAN ARTISTS

The purpose of this chapter is to showcase the work of eight other Alaskan bead artists. The criterion for selection was simple; they are all friends and acquaintances whose work I admire. I asked each to submit one or two pieces, particularly those that reflect the use of Alaskan themes or materials.

Alaska, being somewhat isolated from the Lower 48, has a long, rich tradition of beadwork in its history. I believe modern Alaskan bead artists are producing many interesting and innovative pieces, which will inspire others.

DONNA AFFINITO • PALMER, ALASKA

"Butterfly Barrette"

untitled amulet bag

Inspired by the beadwork of Jane Hodson, Donna Affinito realized her passion for beads in 1993. Donna frequently shares her passion with students of Palmer High School, where she is a guidance secretary. Basketry is another interest, but she always goes back to beads, and often combines beads and basketry.

Donna's blue-ribbon-winning amulet bag was inspired by a new outfit that needed a piece of jewelry. The bag was done in tubular and flat peyote stitch with size 11 beads and accented with twisted fringe. The butterfly barrette was the product of an ugly, rainy, winter day, where an indoor activity, such as sorting beads seemed appropriate. All the bits and pieces that Donna discovered were used in the back-stitched barrette.

"Fire and Icicles"

"Sitting on the Dock of the Bay"

Nine years ago Ruby Brooke purchased a beaded amethyst bola from an artist named Wanda. That purchase fired her obsession with beads, which she happily shares with others at classes, retreats, and the newly formed Alaska Bead Society, Anchorage Chapter.

Lively, fiery beads purchased at Embellishment '96, a class taught by Jeannette Cook, and icicle-like fingers during early morning play with beads were the inspiring ingredients for "Fire and Icicles." The tranquil waters, teeming with oceanic life forms, of Homer, Alaska, as well as beads purchased from several Alaskan bead makers, resulted in "Sitting on the Dock of the Bay".

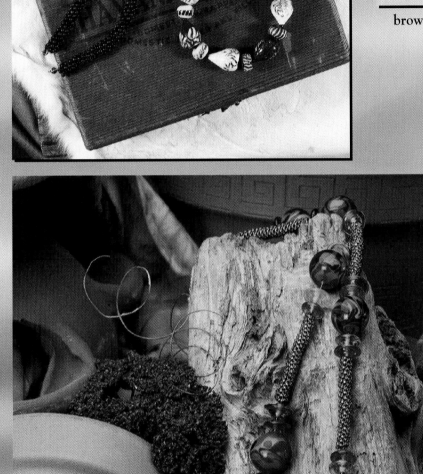

brown/ivory necklace

J ana Coffey's life typifies the "Alaskan Dream". She grew up on a homestead on the Kenai Peninsula, which was only accessible by floatplane. Her present home in beautiful Girdwood Valley is surrounded by seven awe-inspiring glaciers. In 1969 as an art student, Jana was first introduced to hot glass. Having been a serious bead collector for many years, it was only natural that the interest in hot glass and beads would eventually lead to handmade lampwork beads.

Both of these pieces combine seed beads worked in tubular peyote stitch with Jana's handmade beads. The brown and ivory beads are made of imported Italian Morreti glass. Seven large lampwork beads and 28 small multi-colored discs form the focal point of the blue/green necklace.

blue/green necklace

Moosehide Pouch

Tufted Jewelry Box

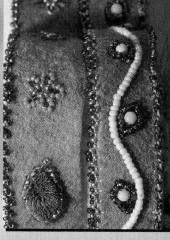

Originally from Koyukuk, Alaska, Lillian DeWilde, an Athabascan Indian, has lived in Fairbanks the past 12 years. She spends her summers at a fish camp called Bishop Mountain. Years ago Lillian's grandmother, Madeline Solomon of Galena, taught her to do beadwork. These days Lillian's bead-working skills supplement the family income. Her spouse Lee and three children, Shawn, Shelly and Rachel, are often found occupying the craft table with Lillian.

Lillian's penchant for combining traditional and contemporary materials is evident in these two pieces. Both are made of smoked moosehide and deer skin, accented with porcupine quilling and tufted caribou/reindeer hair. Note the use of the contemporary beads: Swarovski crystals, Czech glass, and cloisonné. The stitches include edging, couching, and back stitch.

untitled bracelet

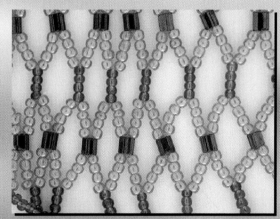

untitled collar

Since 1991 Jane Hodson, whose titles include spouse, homemaker, mother and grandmother, has filled her spare time with beads and basketry, particularly pine needle and antler-accented reed. Jane says she attends Jeanette's beading classes for the "lessons, laughter, and lots of beads." Jane's effervescent personality and hilarious tales definitely contribute to the ambiance.

Jane's bracelet was done on a loom using size 11 beads. The beadwork was then attached to a leather-backed metal bracelet cuff. The motif was inspired by the work of an elderly bead artist in Glenallen, Alaska. Size 11 beads and Czech glass crystals compose the collar, which combines a chevron chain with vertical netting.

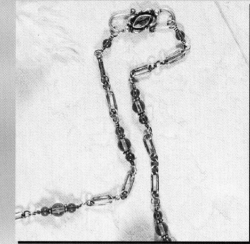

"Beaded Bead Necklace"

"Fairy Amulet Pouch"

Teri Packel has been buying beads as long as she can remember; she readily admits that she's hooked, addicted, obsessed. Good thing, that she works at Black Elk Leather and Beads, Alaska's largest bead store. For Teri beadwork is not only a time filler during long Alaskan winters, but also an outlet for her creative energies. After years of crafting, Teri finally feels she has the right to call herself an artist.

The "Beaded Bead Necklace" consists of Czech glass beads and three peyote-stitched wooden beads, connected with spiral rope and sterling silver chain. Inspired by her daughter Lesley's love of fairies, Teri created the "Fairy Amulet Pouch" depicting a tiny forest fairy. Done in two-drop peyote stitch, the pouch is accented with twisted fringe.

"1997 Love Stamp Amulet Bag"

J acqueline Poston began beading in April 1995 and looks forward to pursuing this passion at all possible free moments. Jacqueline works as an environmental engineer and raises two sons. Jacqueline has lived in Alaska for the past ten years and believes doing beadwork is the best way to spend the long, dark winters!

The "1997 Love Stamp Amulet Bag" is a beaded replica of the US Postal Service stamp. It was completed in tubular peyote stitch with three layers of fringe work. The "Tidal Pool Necklace" consists of back stitching surrounding a lampwork bead by Andrea Guarino of Port Townsend, Washington. The free-form design represents the marine life typically found in a tidal pool.

"Tidal Pool Necklace"

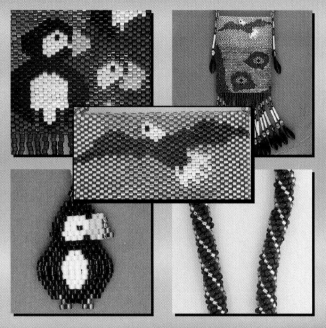

"Baggin' Tourists"

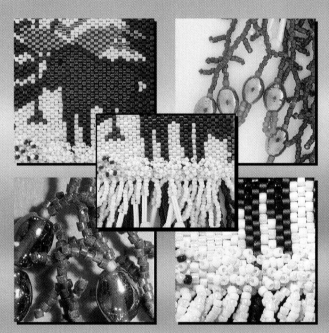

"Moose Nugget Factory"

Tourists flock to Alaska, lured by the certainty of seeing the whimsical puffin, the tail-flapping whale, the cute sea otter, and the soaring bald eagle. "Baggin Tourists," done with delica beads in tubular peyote stitch and spiral weave, echoes the wildlife and beauty of the Kenai Fjords.

Every Alaskan resident, even the urban ones, expects to share his property with the wildlife, especially the moose and bears. The neighborhood moose kindly leave behind droppings, which are gathered, lacquered, and sold to tourists as novelty items. It was tempting to accent this peyote-stitched amulet bag, entitled "Moose Nugget Factory," with real moose nuggets. However, I decided that nugget-shaped, brown glass beads would just be nicer to wear!

Chris Arend photo

"In Full Bloom"

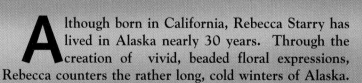

Although born in California, Rebecca Starry has lived in Alaska nearly 30 years. Through the creation of vivid, beaded floral expressions, Rebecca counters the rather long, cold winters of Alaska. She prefers labor-intensive pieces because of the meditative nature of the work. Eight years ago Rebecca was introduced to beadwork by her friend Ruby Brooke. Rebecca is vice-president of the Alaska Bead Society, Anchorage Chapter.

"In Full Bloom" was constructed with Czech seed beads, glass accent beads, and an ivory clasp, using thread and wire to do brick stitch and horizontal square stitch, a stitch which Rebecca developed. Michelle Waldren, an Alaskan bead maker, created the bead used at the center of the three-dimensional daisy.

ABOUT THE AUTHOR

Jeanette Shanigan has been an admitted bead addict for the past ten years. She has been trying to hook others through beadwork classes for the past six years. Because of the stresses associated with her job of high school teacher, Jeanette knows an avenue of escape is vital. Jeanette believes that beadwork can relieve stress, as well as satisfy the creative urges inherent in us all. Beadwork serves an added purpose for Jeanette and her fellow Alaskan bead addicts: it helps speed the passage of those long, dark winter months! She is a member of the Alaska Bead Society, Anchorage Chapter. Jeanette lives with her spouse and two sons in Wasilla, Alaska.

INDEX